What was it like in the Concentration Camp at Dachau?

An attempt to come closer to the truth

by

Dr. Johannes Neuhäusler, † 1973
Auxiliary Bishop of Munich

Translated from the German

24th Edition

September 1993

Trustees for the Monument of Atonement
in the Concentration Camp at Dachau
c/o Karmel Hl. Blut · D-85221 Dachau
Alte Römerstraße 91 · Postscheckkonto München 76766-809

Published by Manz A.G., Munich/Dillingen
Clichés: Osiris Cliché Factory, Munich 5

Introduction

"If the miracle should happen, that you live to tell the tale, write it down and tell the world what they did to us."

"That was the most sacred will of the comrades who died in our arms or were removed by the 'invalids-transport' to be gassed. That was the will of brothers and true friends, of the 'number-men' (Nummermenschen, the men who seemed to have no names, but only numbers), whose ashes escaped through the chimneys and covered the fields of a foreign country."

It was this dying wish expressed by men who were his fellow-prisoners in Dachau which moved the Polish writer, *Jan Domagala,* to set about investigating and collecting evidence about Dachau, the first of all German concentration camps and their prototype. It was this last request which bade him, who had escaped with his life after many years' imprisonment, to take the pen in hand, and write his book, *,Ci, którzy przeszli przez Dachau'* "Those Who Went Through Dachau" (Warsaw – Pax 1957).

This well-documented work is the fruit of several years' study of painstakingly-collected statistics and we owe its translation to the kindness of the Salvatorian, Father Angelus Siebert. Together with Franz Goldschmitt's *Zeugen des Abendlandes* ("Western Witnesses", published by Felten-Verlag, Saarlouis) it seemed to me to be a particularly trustworthy source for a factual account of Dachau.

Naturally, I also used other publications on the concentration camp at Dachau and I drew on my own limited experience. After several months' imprisonment in the Gestapo prisons in Munich and Berlin and after two months in the concentration camp at Sachsenhausen-Oranienburg, I was sent to Dachau on July 12, 1941 and remained there until April 24, 1945. I was what was known as a *"special prisoner"* and was confined in the "Bunker" (the jail of the Dachau concentration camp). Thus separated from the general camp, I could not learn all that happened there. I did, however, see and hear much that happened in the "Dark Cells" and the "Standing Cells" of the bunker and especially, what happened in the yard during the first year.

3

No one person, however, even if he had been in Dachau from the day it opened to the day it was closed, could know the *whole* truth about it, nor give a complete answer to the question which is so often asked: *"What was it like in Dachau?"* Still less could he answer such questions as: *"How many were imprisoned in Dachau?"* (from 1933 to 1945), or *"Who died in Dachau?"* or *"Who were their torturers and executioners?"*

The answers to these and similar questions differ greatly. Thus, estimates of the number of deaths in Dachau vary enormously. *Zauner,* the retired mayor of Dachau, put it at 20,600, Pastor *Niemöller* (quoting an inscription written in Dachau in 1945) at 238,756. *Slew Gardner* named a similar figure (230,000) in an article in the *Sunday Express* on 10 January, 1960.

Why this great lack of certainty and the enormous differences between the estimates? Is it due to a lack of willingness to speak the truth, to feel and confess guilt, to be accurate and honest?

I do not believe so. The root of the evil seems to me to lie much deeper: in the *great secrecy* which surrounded the concentration camp at Dachau from the very beginning to the end, as was the case with all concentration camps and all other such extermination centres of the Third Reich.

"Evil loves the darkness and hates the light". Fog, impenetrable fog, lay upon the camp at Dachau during twelve years. Neither those who lived nearby nor the people of Dachau could penetrate this fog of secrecy. How often did I try to learn something from individual released prisoners. It was all in vain. They were silent and asked not to be questioned further. It could have meant new danger to life to talk about it. Indeed, it could have meant the immediate return of the ex-prisoner to Dachau. Every outsider who dared to speak about it could be brought to jail, even if he spoke only the truth, as was the case with the city pastor *Dr. Emil Muhler* of Munich and two of his assistant priests. I, myself, experienced this too. Because I informed the Holy Father and the Bishops about the National Socialistic injustice and wrong-doings I had to be "cooled off", as the Gestapo expressed it.

Father Franz Goldschmitt, whose *Zeugen des Abendlandes* we have already mentioned, was in Dachau from 16 December, 1942 to the end of May, 1945 – until after the liberation, that is. In the foreword to his book he says: "I made notes secretly, very secretly, the rope already tightening around my neck, for whoever was caught collecting information against the National Socialists was hanged". (For details of the Nazis' methods of hiding their activities behind a smoke-screen, see my book *Kreuz und Hakenkreuz*, Munich 1946, Part II, page 12 ff.). And even after the gates of this notorious camp were forced open on April 29, 1945, the truth about this hotbed of

4

crime and slavery did not appear for a long time, for much that could have been shown to the world, in names and numbers, the kind of inhumanities and cruelties committed within its walls, *had been destroyed in the last moments by those responsible for the atrocities.*

So it was that much was concealed, denied or minimised and declared mere Allied war propaganda. The words: "Don't make much fuss about it! Let grass grow over it!" were heard in public and in private.

And it is for that the world justly blames us. If we do not make the truth known, we commit a new injustice against those who died in the concentration camps, whose last request was *"Tell what they did to us!"* If we do not discover the truth, we deprive ourselves of the lessons which these deplorable happenings can teach us, and we thus expose ourselves to new dangers. "Only the truth will make us free" (John 8, 32). It will allow us to say a sincere "mea culpa" before God and our neighbours and urge us to make atonement and reparation.

We Germans also have to make our own the words expressed by some Englishmen as they looked upon the atrocities committed in the Third Reich:

"We will forgive but not forget".

Or, as has been said more forcefully in a discussion of Edmond Michelet's Rue de la Liberté ("Street of Liberty"): "No one who reads about it will be temped *to forget* what kind of place Dachau was. *But in his heart the Christian has already forgiven."*

This sentiment must guide us Germans also. Since hatred and revenge should be strangers to us, we are willing to forgive in Christian love all those who did wrong through wickedness, delusion or seduction; but we must not forget the abysses of satanic wickedness and ungodliness to which those men sank who had been voted full power by the German people. And we may not and will not forget to what dechristianisation leads, how man is degraded when he loses faith in God and thinks he is not responsible to a higher authority. He really can become a beast, a devil.

Faith cannot highly enough exalt the dignity of man, hence it says to the Creator:

"What is man that Thou art mindful of him?
Or the son of man that Thou visitest him?
Thou hast made him a little less than the angels: Thou hast crowned him with glory and honour.
Thou hast set him over the works of Thy hands, and subjected all things under his feet." (Psalm 8)

Disbelief, however, can lower man to the level of a beast, to a mere thing and a number, can ill-treat him pitilessly, yes, even murder him and destroy the corpse. The pen should strive against the writer even to describe sordid facts, to describe them fully in their awful cruelty and inhumanity; yet for the sake of truth and as a warning, nothing must be suppressed or forgotten.

Dachau can and shall be a lesson! Therefore, we dare not be silent about it, although the memory of it is sad and grievous.

And likewise we will not forget what those endured who suffered for their convictions, chiefly for their faith in God, for their fidelity to the Church, even for their freedom and for the rights of all of us. Although all might not have been innocent personally, yet they had to suffer immoderately in body and soul.

With the memorial chapel which was dedicated on the occasion of the 37th International Eucharistic Congress (the dedication took place on August 5, 1960) before the eyes of the whole world, we will not only honour those who suffered there, but also make a place where prayers and the Holy Sacrifice may be offered up to God for the misdeeds of the torturers.

"Forgive, but do not forget!"

Let this be the recurring thought throughout the following statements. For this reason practically no names or persons will be mentioned; facts and happenings will be reported as reliably as they could be found. We will leave the trial and punishment of crimes to the courts of justice. Conscious that I cannot give a report which is 100% accurate or 100% complete, I call this book "an *attempt* to come closer to the truth".

Well aware that others have seen and experienced far more than I, I let them speak for themselves. I shall be grateful for every correction and supplement.

Munich, June 17, 1960

Johann Neuhäusler, Auxiliary Bishop
Prisoner in Sachsenhausen No. 37 796
Prisoner in Dachau No. 26 680

I. The Concentration Camp at Dachau. When did it begin? Who was responsible for its existence?

On March 21, 1933 the following announcement appeared in the paper *Münchner Neuesten Nachrichten:*

"On Wednesday, March 22, 1933, the first concentration camp will be opened in the vicinity of Dachau. It can accommodate 5,000 people. We have adopted this measure, undeterred by paltry scruples, in the conviction that our action will help to restore calm to our country and is in the best interests of our people.

Heinrich Himmler
Commissioner of Police for the city of Munich."

With this announcement the first concentration camp of the Third Reich was established.

Dachau

is more than nine miles northwest of Munich. Its history goes back more than a thousand years. The counts of Dachau, ancestors of the Wittelsbachers, enjoyed a good reputation far and wide for hundreds of years.

The concentration camp which, from 1933 to 1945 and in the post-war years, stained the name of Dachau in the eyes of the entire world, did not really form a part of Dachau but of Prittlbach.

The main part of the camp served as a munition factory during World War I. In 1937/38 the camp was enlarged, the new barracks and administration buildings were erected. The old halls of the former munition factory were not pulled down but were used as workshops. Located in a former swamp, Dachau has a poor climate, moist and foggy — truly a waste land.

Certainly, in the course of the years, beautiful walks, gardens and flower-beds were made by the prisoners and fertilized by their sweat and blood! This beauty of nature, facing the Alps, which were sometimes visible in their majestic splendour, the magnificent sunrise and sunset which were sometimes visible during the long morning and evening roll-calls, greatly contributed as Domagala says, to the psychical dejection of the prisoners and made them sigh: "My God, how beautiful is Thy world! But my fellowmen keep me from enjoying it. And will not my life disappear like this dawn and this sunset at the command of Hitler?"

II. A walk through Hitler's large prison

The concentration camp was rectangular being about 990 feet wide and 1980 feet long. West of it the formation camp of the SS-men was located. From this building a wide asphalt street led to the prison camp:

"The turnpike to hell"

The camp guard house, called the "Jourhaus", was at the end of this street. The large iron gate of this building bore the inscription:

„Arbeit macht frei" (*"Work makes you free"*)

The irony of it! A more fitting inscription would habe been: "Forget what you were! Now you are slaves." Still better would have been the words which Dante wrote in his *Divine Comedy* above the entrance to hell: "Give up all hope, you who enter here!"

The same irony, the same untruth and mockery marked another inscription which greeted the prisoners from the roof of the administration building:

„Es gibt einen Weg zur Freiheit.
Seine Meilensteine heißen:
Gehorsam – Fleiß – Ehrlichkeit – Ordnung –
Sauberkeit – Nüchternheit – Wahrheit –
Opfersinn und Liebe zum Vaterland."

"There is one road to freedom.
Its milestones are:
Obedience – diligence – honesty – order –
Cleanliness – temperance – truthfulness –
Sacrifice and love of one's country."

The authors seemed to have been unconscious of the bitter irony of the passage. They were unaware of their own complete lack of the qualities they prescribed.

The exterior and interior construction of the camp showed German thoroughness and skilful organisation. However, all did not serve for the welfare of the inmates but only to assure their slavery and degradation and frequently their execution. We could say:

"Well organised
to command and rule,
to torture and murder!"
"Satan had erected his throne here" (Apocalypse 2, 13)

Let us enter his camp residence, the

"Jourhaus".

The upper floor was occupied by the SS-authorities, the camp leader and his deputies and here also were the offices of the Gestapo trial commissioner. The offices of the report leader and the guardroom were on the ground-floor.

The administration offices

comprised also large storage rooms for the personal belongings of the prisoners. There was a large shower installation for about 150 persons, a large kitchen with modern equipment, a cellar, a laundry and a clothes-store.

The bunker

From the "Jourhaus" a street led to the bunker. This street was infamous. The prisoners had often to stand here for several hours in rainy weather, frost and heat for the least violation of rules.

From the offices a passage led through flowerbeds to the

roll-call square.

Day after day the dreaded morning and evening roll-calls took place here, and here, too, in the presence of all the prisoners, corporal punishment was inflicted, especially on those who had attempted to escape. From here the labour gangs marched away every day to their work and returned again at night with a song on their lips! Sometimes they even marched back to the music of the camp-band. Here, too, prisoners were paraded naked and from them were chosen the candidates for the "invalids-transport" to be taken to the gas chambers. Prisoners who felt ill would stand here helplessly before the report leader after roll-call and ask to be assigned to the sick quarters. This square also served for recreation on Sundays if it was granted as a special concession; here the prisoners had to listen to the loud speakers shouting out the "victories of Hitler". Leading from this square was a wonderful tree-lined street about 990 feet long and 99 feet wide. Here, thirty barracks, the living quarters of the prisoners, were located. Michelet ironically calls it "Street of Liberty".

The Canteen

The canteen of the SS-men was served by the prisoners. Here, cigarettes and sometimes food, such as beet-jam, oatmeal biscuits, cucumbers pickled in wood-vinegar, raw sauerkraut, sour carrots, snails and the like, all very expensive and not very good, were sold. Nevertheless, everything was readily devoured by the starving prisoners.

The Museum

The museum containing plaster images of prisoners who were marked by bodily defects or particular characteristics was gladly visited by Hitler's officers. At one time they were not content with this exhibition of plaster images alone, and so the officers and visitors to the camp were led to the prisoners' bunker where distinguished persons, church dignitaries of various confessions, such as Bishop Kozal, political figures from conquered countries, well-known artists and politicians were presented. The officers used to laugh and scoff at these prisoners and often violently lay hands upon them.

The Camp Office

in which the prisoners worked had files on all prisoners of the main camp as well as on all "Out Commands". There was also a card-index of the deceased and of those who had been transferred to other camps or released. In the camp office the mail was distributed to each block. The camp secretary together with the block secretary made regular reports and submitted them to the camp leader. Interpreters in various languages were also engaged in the office. By using the card-index the transport lists of prisoners who had been selected by the SS-men for transfer to other camps were made out. In agreement with the SS-men the *labour office* assigned prisoners to various occupations both inside and outside the camp.

The library

was well equipped with various books which were procured "cheaply" – that is, simply confiscated from the prisoners. It was used very much especially after 1942 when some provision for free time was introduced.

The Living Quarters

The barracks on the left side were numbered two to thirty and were occupied by the working prisoners. Two, and later, five barracks on the right side were used for the

Infirmary.

Some of those in the infirmary were prisoners who had been so weakened that they were no longer able to stand, others had been brought there by friendly fellow prisoners. Prisoners staffed the infirmary. Some of them were army surgeons. Others were persons of different nationalities, who knew practically nothing about the care of the sick. From 1942 onward imprisoned physicians were also allowed to assist in the infirmary. The medical staff was headed by the infirmary Capo on whom the treatment of the patient depended. A perverse infirmary Capo would do away with sick prisoners without telling the SS doctor on duty, using injections and tortures of his own devising.

Besides modern hospital equipment, the infirmary had also a dental treatment room. It was exhibited to "Hitler's officers" and to foreign visitors, who admired it greatly.

In the infirmary office files were kept on the sick and dead. Behind this were other rooms in which bodies were dissected to ascertain the cause of death. In the reports, the cause of death was always given as "heart attack and embolism". There was also a mortuary in which bodies and human skeletons were preserved. When there was no more room here, the bodies were piled up on the street and then hauled off to the crematorium. Prisoners loaded them like sacks of flour upon the so-called "Moor-express", especially in the last months when an outbreak of typhoid claimed a hundred and more victims daily.

Quarantine

Later, single barracks were set aside for invalids or those affected with itch or – as was the case in the last phase of the camp – for victims of spotted fever.

The barrack of the convict company

After some years, Barrack number fifteen became known as the block where the severest punishment was meted out. Here the so-called "convict company" was housed. It consisted chiefly of *Jews*, but also included prisoners who had tried to escape and prisoners who had violated camp regulations.

11

North

Norden

zum Krematorium

To the crematorium

West · Westen

East · Osten

Süden

South

Key:

1 Watch-towers
2 Bunker (jail)
3 Bunker for the SS-convicts
4 Effects chamber (dressing room, shoemaker, tailor, mending room)
5 Bureau for management of private property of the prisoners
6 Bath-room, kitchen, laundry, also room for punishment
7 Entrance gate, above it the "Jourhaus"
8/9 Roll-call square
10 Camp street, right and left each 17 living barracks. In the first two blocks on the west side: canteen, library and school-room; on the east side the "infirmary", later enlarged to five blocks. B, C, D, E and the numbering 1—30 indicate the barracks.
11 Garden management
12 Hutch for rabbits (to get angora wool for the pilots)
13 Disinfection barracks
14 The Catholic "Agony of Christ Chapel" built in 1960.
15 The Protestant "Church of Reconciliation", completed in 1967.
16 The Jewish Memorial, built in 1967.
17 The Carmelite Convent of the "Precious Blood", built in 1964.

Description of the living accommodation

The living quarters were divided into blocks, each of which was three hundred and thirty feet long by thirty-three feet wide. Each block was divided into two parts and each part had its separate entrance. (See plan.)

Dormitory IV	Living-room	W.C.	Wash-r.	Living-room III	Dormitory	Dormitory II	Living-room	W.C.	Wash-r.	Living-room I	Dormitory	Camp Street

In the normal pattern, the main entrance gave access to two apartments, each containing a living-room and a dormitory. Forty-five wardrobes lined the walls of the living-room, one for each prisoner. There was the same number of chairs and four tables. There were forty-five beds in the dormitory, one row of beds above the other. They were arranged so that they could accommodate ninety persons, the prisoners of two apartments. At first one block or barrack was supposed to accommodate one hundred and eighty persons (forty-five in each of the four apartments), the entire camp 5,000 persons. (Later, two hundred and more were frequently housed in one apartment.) At first, especially during the period before the war, an *SS block-leader* was in charge of each block. Later, however, one man had to take charge of several barracks and blocks. In each block, one of the prisoners, called the *"block senior"*, was put in charge. He was responsible to the SS-man. The *"apartment senior"*, the block secretary, the barber and the manager of the canteen were in turn responsible to the "block senior".

Overcrowded conditions

As we said at the beginning, the camp at Dachau provided lodgings for 5,000 prisoners, but after 1942 the number of prisoners was never less than 12,000.

Communists, leading Socialists and other "enemies of the state" were the chief arrests in 1933. They erected more barracks. Large transports of German Jews began to arrive at the camp from November 1938 onward. After a short term of imprisonment, most of them received permission to go overseas, especially when they "voluntarily" gave all their property to enrich Hitler's public treasury.

After the annexation of *Austria* and the conquest of *Czechoslovakia* the citizens of these countries were the next victims and prisoners of the con-

13

centration camp at Dachau. In the year 1940 large transports of Polish prisoners came to Dachau and while the camp lasted the Poles constituted the largest number of prisoners. There were also large and small groups of other nationalities. On April 26, 1945 the number of prisoners amounted to a total of about 30,000 *men* in the main camp, that is, in Dachau itself.

The overcrowding of the camp is shown in a terrifying manner by the following report of the number of prisoners in single living-blocks on April 26, 1945. Instead of the foreseen regular number of 180 men for each block there were in

Block 2	939 mostly Germans		Block 18	1138 Poles
Block 4	842 mostly Germans		Block 20	1152 Czechs and others
Block 6	1403 Russians		Block 22	1446 Russians and others
Block 8	1356 from various nations		Block 24	1146 from various nations
Block 10	1117 from various nations		Block 26	1090 Priests and others
Block 12	1140 Serbians, Slovenes		Block 28	1547 from various nations
Block 14	990 from various nations		Block 30	1800 especially sick an
Block 16	1137 Poles			invalids

Precautions taken to prevent escape

A piece of ground measuring ten feet wide called the *"neutral-zone"* was around all the camp buildings and it was strictly forbidden to trespass on this area. A *ditch,* four feet deep and about eight feet broad, lay behind it. The whole concentration camp was fenced with *barbed* wire which was charged with electricity, and by a wall. Close behind the wires on the west side, the camp was surrounded by a deep canal filled with water. It was connected with the river Amper which flows west of the camp at a distance of about 1,650 feet.

Watch towers

were erected at the most important points and at the corners and these were manned by the SS. From one of them, the already mentioned "Jourhaus", the shrill voice of the SS-officer, always a trial to the prisoners' ears, sounded: "Tower A no incidents". Meanwhile, scenes reminiscent of Dante took place in the proximity of the tower, beating, kicking, ill-treatment and murdering of the prisoners, the admittance of transports of prisoners, many of whom were half dead, and others who were earmarked for immediate extermination.

Machine guns were mounted on the towers, their barrels directed towards the camp. At every movement in the "neutral-zone" or in the vicinity of

14

the ditch and barbed wire fence shots came from the watch-towers without any warning and the prisoner who was in this zone was "put down" at once. It often happened that prisoners in a state of madness and despair threw themselves against the wire at night and died there.

Our description of the concentration camp would not be complete without mention of the barracks and building *outside the barbed wire fence* but yet close by and with which the prisoners also came in direct or indirect contact. To these the office of the

<h2 style="text-align:center">political section</h2>

belonged. The fate of the prisoners was decided there. Orders for discharging came from there but also orders for the execution of individual prisoners or entire groups. Further details of personal files of the prisoners were preserved there too. In agreement with the camp commandant, mostly negative reports were given when a higher authority requested information about the prisoners' conduct.

The political section was in reality the prolongation of the arm of the Gestapo within the territory of the camp.

The Crematorium

Also behind the wire fence was the *camp crematorium*. At first it was housed in a wooden barrack, later in a stone building built by Polish Catholic priests, to whom the building trade had been taught. This crematorium was located in a small forest on the west side quite close to the camp.

The prevailing wind was from the west and, consequently, the smell of burning corpses filled the camp, reminding the prisoners of their approaching end and adding immeasurably to their despair.

With the new crematorium a

gas chamber

was also connected. The whole construction of the crematorium with its gas chamber was completed in 1943. It contained an "undressing room", a "shower bath", and a "mortuary". The "showers" were metal traps which had no pipelines for a supply of poisonous gas. This gas chamber was never set in action in Dachau. Only the dead were brought to the crematorium for "burning", no living for "gassing". And yet thousands of the inmates of Dachau were gassed. For this purpose they were brought

15

as "Invalids-Transport" (from 1942–1944 alone, 3166 prisoners) to Hartheim, near Linz (Austria). (See page 29)

Michelet reports ("Street of Liberty", page 200) about a good use for the gas chamber and for the poison gas provided. When an epidemic of typhoid fever broke out in the camp in the winter of 1944, the Capo of the disinfection commando suggested to the camp leader that they use the cyclone gas to disinfect the rags and tatters which lay in heaps in the yard of the disinfection barracks and were dangerous bearers of lice. The experiment proved to be a successful undertaking. However, the gas chamber was not used for this. Instead small rooms, situated at the western exit of the crematorium, as well as one other camp-building used generally for disinfection, served this purpose.

III. The big and little dictators of the concentration camp

"I am not the Lord God. Why are you standing there as if you wanted to pray?", so I heard a troop leader in the Sachsenhausen concentration camp say to a fellow-priest-prisoner when he, at the sudden appearance of the troop leader, held his hand over his stomach, in order to hide the fact that he had a book under his jacket. (It was not allowed at that time to read except during the specified time.) "Yes, I am not the Lord God!" That certainly was right but all camp commandants certainly behaved as if they were the Lord God.

As head of the main camp and the working camp stood the

camp commandant.

Some of the commandants were not a all interested in the affairs of the prisoners and gave full power to their deputies, the camp leaders. I mention the commandant *Weiss* out of gratitude and as a proof that among the despots of the concentration camp there were also some with human feelings. He introduced many pleasant changes in the camp and checked personally if his regulations and orders were observed. He forbade the deliberate beating of the prisoners by the Capos and camp seniors, he personally inspected criminal reports, he himself determined the punishment and was present when it was carried out, lest abuses were introduced. He also removed an abuse, namely, that the prisoners had to be close-cropped and had to have a still shorter strip, the so-called "path" in the middle of the head. To preserve the prisoners' strength for the armaments industry, Weiss permitted them to receive food parcels which made it possible for a large number of prisoners to keep alive in the camp until the end. Often he also showed a fundamentally good heart to us "special prisoners" and procured manifold

Father Leisner
ordained
in the camp
at Dachau

A wooden monstrance covered with tin;
it was made by the Salesian Father Schmidt.

Preceding page:
Above: Crematorium of the concentration
camp
Below: Cemetery on the Leitenberg near
Dachau (for about 7.500 prisoners). –
Photo: Tögel

facilities for us. In the last phase he became inspector of the concentration camps. Because he foresaw the complete collapse of Hitler's power, he did not permit the carrying out of Himmler's command to shell and burn the camp at Dachau together with all its inmates on the night of 28/29 April, 1945. (Yet he was tragically sentenced to death and executed by the Allies after the war, presumably because he signed and executed death sentences which came from Berlin.)

The Camp Leader

The camp leader was responsible for the numerical stability of the prisoners, for the criminal procedures and the realisation of the daily programmes. In the years 1940–1942, the SS-Hauptsturmführer Z. (chief storm leader) was camp leader and he was famous for his brutality. His "merit" consisted in the severe punishment of the prisoners, without good reasons, for insignificant transgressions and without any, even the least, possibility of defence or explanation. He particularly liked the punishment at the stake (in the camp it was called the "tree") and the flogging with at least twenty-five lashes.

The Report Leader

One of the most important assistants of the camp-leader was the report-leader. He was responsible for the preparation of the reports on stability and executed the orders and regulations of the camp-leader. He came into immediate contact with the prisoners. Domagala's description of some of the report-leaders is, simply, "camp beasts". They took pleasure in playing tricks on the prisoners everywhere and on every occasion. Beating, kicking and ill-treatment of their charges were part of their daily schedule.

To carry out their policies, these camp-leaders and report-leaders had the service of certain

block-leaders.

Until the year 1940 they were chosen from particular confidants of the SS-men. In the course of time they were raised to the rank of officer and practised the functions of camp-leaders. Towards the end of 1944 they were replaced by non-commissioned officers who were unfit for service on the front. The latter often made friends with the prisoners, especially when they received part of the contents of the food parcels. At times they were even opposed to the SS-men. Nevertheless, eighty per cent of them were zealous "cyclists" – crawling to authorities, walking on inferiors.

17

E. Michelet ("Street of Liberty", p. 137) relates an example of the sadism with which the block-leaders could carry out the mocking and degrading of the prisoners: When the police officer, Captain Veyssières, arrived at the camp, the SS-men took away all his belongings, leaving him only his cap and sword-belt. One day as he was taking a "shower" the block-leader took away all his prison clothes. As he was entirely naked and possessed only the two non-essential accessories, the derision began at once; ten times, jes, twenty times, Veyssières had to run in front of the dismayed prisoners. "Hurry up, hurry up!", the SS-man cried and began to laugh loudly and beat his thighs for pleasure. Finally, when he could stand it no longer, Veyssières threw himself in a rage and full of shame before his comrades who stood there with gritted teeth.

Another example of perversity is told by Goldschmitt (page 30): "We frequently heard of the following disgusting ill-treatment. An order was given: 'In double-quick time, take up your position!' As they pass, the prisoners receive many kicks. The second order was: 'In two rows take up your position facing each other! Attention! Punch one another in the face!' Nobody does it. 'Do it at once!' No one moves. Instead of paying tribute to the prisoners' comradeship, the wild ruffians pushed two comrades against each other so that their heads struck and began to bleed. Then the hangman's assistants go through the rows and beat the prisoners in the face with their fists. 'If you had beaten one another, jou would have been better off', says one now in an insolent tone. Then comes another order: 'Again take your position in two rows facing each other. Spit upon each other in the face!' Nobody obeys. The pistols are cocked. 'For the last time I order you to spit at each other . . .' Now, some spat but scarcely perceptibly. Then the SS-swine came forward and hurled thick flat cakes of spittle into the faces of the prisoners. The prisoners have to lick each other clean now."

The Interrogation Officer

We still have to say a word about the interrogation officer B., who was subordinate to the camp-leaders. He distinguished himself by his particular zeal and repeatedly demanded death sentences for so-called "sabotages". B. made use of a criminal in the camp as his "confidential prisoner" who told him everything that was said and done in the block apartments. In this way he contributed to the punishment of many fellow-prisoners.

The Camp Seniors

Neither the report-leader nor the block-leader always remained in the camp; they lived outside the camp territory. However, for understandable reasons, a specially appointed camp senior was always present in the camp, *a prisoner* who was the superior of the block seniors. Thousands of tragedies, plunderings, murders and intrigues were the work of these same "seniors".

18

The Block Seniors

As the camp-leader had a camp senior as his assistant, so a block-leader was assisted by a block senior who again commanded four apartment seniors. General disciplinary regulations and the camp-leader's circulars were passed on by the camp-leaders and block-seniors. Unfortunately, many of these were criminals of the worst type.

But among them were men who identified themselves completely with their fellow-prisoners and pleaded for them, for instance, *Scherer* and more especially *Karl Wagner*.

The following incident is an example of Karl Wagner's loyalty to a fellow-prisoner. When he became camp-senior in the affiliated camp at Allach in 1944, the camp-leader wanted to force him to flog one of his fellow-prisoners publicly in front of the other prisoners. Wagner refused, took the band denoting his position as camp-senior from his arm and placed it upon the wooden trestle upon which he should have flogged a fellow-prisoner. After this incident he lost his position as camp senior, was placed in the bunker for three months, and was then brought back into the camp at Dachau.

The Block Secretary

All matters of administration rested upon the shoulders of the block secretary. Reports on stability and nutrition, lists, mail, arrangements etc. had to be submitted to him. The block secretary was subordinate to the camp head clerk from whom he received all orders and instructions. Prisoners who were camp-functionaries were treated in the same way as the other prisoners. The SS-men saw in them only creatures who were not allowed to think for themselves; for the smallest transgression they were beaten in the face at once or punished in various ways as was customary in the camp.

After the liberation, lists were made in the camp office of all prisoners who died during the entire time of the existence of the camp; identification cards for the prisoners were issued and other statistics were prepared.

Up to eighty per cent of the prisoners who were employed in the camp office and of those who acted as block secretaries were men who tried to save the prisoners in every respect and to bring them facilities wherever possible, regardless of their nationality, political views etc. Often they came in conflict even with the SS-authorities and the block-seniors and camp-seniors. In the later years, when things were difficult at the front, the various camp-functionaries gained such influence that they succeeded in saving hundreds of prisoners. The board of management in the camp, composed of prisoners, generally functioned very well. The roll-call, taken twice daily, had to be absolutely correct.

The Infirmary Leader

The infirmary was a separate independent administration unit, supervised by the chief SS-physician and withdrawn from the control of the camp leader.

The infirmary Capo was in charge of the infirmary. In the years 1940–1942, this office was held by the prisoner H., who often treated the prisoners in a beastly way. Together with a selected band of inhuman nurses he was at the same time the executing instrument of the SS-men and murdered the prisoners according to all rules of the hangman's art. Prisoners who were not in a completely hopeless condition and who sought medical aid received such blows from him that soon they were fit to be admitted to the infirmary.

The nature of the "specialist" treatment given to the prisoners is shown by the following: Two prisoners dragged a companion who could no longer walk to the infirmary. At the threshold they were reveived by H. They were Poles. One of the prisoners began to explain in broken German that they had brought a sick prisoner who could not walk. H. began his "medical treatment" by checking the sick man carelessly, at the same time crying aloud that this man was in very good condition and could walk by himself. He tried to convince the two prisoners that the patient could move and began to beat and kick him. The sick man could not stand the torture inflicted upon him, he regained consciousness and gathering his last strength together, escaped from the infirmary. He went back to the block and "calmly" breathed his last near the stove. Now, H. seized one of the helpers, ill-treated him, flogged him and asserted that he intended to deceive him by bringing a healthy man to the infirmary. After such ill-treatment this comrade, who up to then had been healthy, was a fit patient for the infirmary.

Here, also, we dare not conceal the fact that among the infirmary leaders and nurses were men who were not wanting in self-sacrifice and who cared for the sick in an exemplary manner.

The Infirmary Office

The infirmary office handled the administrative affairs of the infirmary in connection with the camp office especially in regard to matters of stability and reports on nutrition.

The Labour Exchange

The labour exchange played an important role too. The prisoners employed in this office had alphabetical lists with numbers, professions, and the work assigned to the different groups and commandos. They did what lay in their power to save their comrades from various vexations on the part of individual Capos.

IV. The Dachau Concentration Camp: its inmates

> "Who counts the people, tells the name,
> of those who here as guests together came?"

one would like to repeat, with the poet, changing the phrase "as guests" to "with sorrow". During the years the number of prisoners increased so much that "out-commands" had to be opened, in near-by and outlying districts. Today the museum has a map showing 35 of the most important outlying branch-camps of the Concentration Camp at Dachau. The register of the "International Inquiry Service" from Arolsen records 167 such branch camps.

The camp at Dachau was intended only for *men*, while that at Ravensbrück admitted mostly women.

Father Goldschmitt affirms, however, in his booklet "Alsatians and Lothringians in Dachau" that 5,000 women were among the prisoners liberated by the Americans on April 29, 1945.

Joos relates in his book "Leben auf Widerruf" (Otto Walter Verlag), page 151: "A transport from the Russian-Polish territory brought four women disguised in men's clothes. Were they perhaps women who had followed their husbands? We could never find out. K., the third camp commandant, killed them by shots in the neck."

Father Goldschmitt records for April 27, 1945: "Hundreds of Jews have been crowded into wagons which are still at the depot. The poor people must starve to death; some hundreds of Jewesses who have been wandering about for two days arrive. Many of them are dying from exhaustion" (Page 157/58).

They probably came from other camps and out-commands. During the war with Russia, hundreds of boys whose ages ranged from twelve to fifteen years were in Dachau for some time, and even some seven year-olds were also there. What happened to them nobody knows. Do the children's bones which were found during excavations in the ground of the camp at Dachau not so long ago give the answer?

Terrible Annual Balances

In his book "Those Who Went Through Dachau" Domagala gives the following increases in the number of prisoners annually:

1933	4 821		1940	22 675 (esp. from Poland)
1934	1 990		1941	6 135
1935	2 111		1942	12 572
1936	2 323		1943	19 358
1937	2 015		1944	78 635
1938	18 681 (esp. from Austria)		1945	30 958
1939	3 932 (esp. from Czechoslovakia)			

The total number of prisoners who went through Dachau according to these figures: 206,206.

The Final Balance

Three days before the liberation, that is on April 26, 1945, the final balance according to the report of the camp authorities was as follows:

in the main camp at Dachau	30 442
in the branch camps	37 223
accordingly a total of	67 665

The following table shows the number of prisoners from each country.

1.	Albanians	44	20.	Italians	3 388
2.	Americans	11	21.	Japanese	1
3.	Arabians	3	22.	Latvians	230
4.	Armenians	4	23.	Lithuanians	3 250
5.	Belgians	989	24.	Luxemburgers	211
6.	Bulgarians	54	25.	Norwegians	77
7.	Canadians	1	26.	Persians (Iran)	1
8.	Chinese	2	27.	Poles	14 994
9.	Croats	818	28.	Portuguese	8
10.	Czechs	1 974	29.	Roumanians	69
11.	Danes	1	30.	Russians	13 536
12.	Dutchmen	836	31.	Serbians	516
13.	Englishmen	13	32.	Slovacs	244
14.	Esthonians	5	33.	Slovenes	1 746
15.	Finns	1	34.	Spaniards	286
16.	Frenchmen	5 706	35.	Swedes	7
17.	Germans	6 118	36.	Swiss	12
18.	Greeks	338	37.	Turks	86
19.	Hungarians	12 067	38.	without nationality	17

(The numbers given by Goldschmitt in *Western Witnesses* page 11, are the same except for some small differences.)

The Total Balance of the camp at Dachau from 1933–1945*

Nobody can state the exact number (cfr. Introduction).

A) The *"International Inquiry Service"* from Arolsen (near Waldeck) gives the total number of persons delivered to the camp at Dachau (date May 12, 1960) as follows:

    a) according to the card-index of the office   177 447

    b) variation of the report for the "Action Jews" 1938/39 for which no card-index exists   10 911

                                                188 358

"To this, yet other figures must be added – immense figures, probably – the number of those who had been transferred there a short time before the liberation and who had not been registered. Further, those arrested during 1933 to 1934 were not registered."

B) Jan Domagala tries to calculate the numbers who went through Dachau from the numbering of prisoners. He concludes:

      I. Numbering from 1933–1940   1 to   37 575

     II. Numbering from 1940–1945   1 to 161 944

                  Both numbers added = 199 519

Here, however, we have to consider that at the first numbering any number which was later free, due to death or discharging, was given again, therefore, the total number of prisoners from 1933/40 would have been higher than 37 575.

Numbers

This calculation of the total sum according to the numbers assigned makes it possible for us to know what the prisoner was only a number for the rulers of the Third Reich, and for the camp leader easy to wipe out, easy to substitute. For us, however, each number signifies a vast sea of suffering borne by the prisoner and his relatives. And each year number increased and with it the sufferings too.

Let us read about this in the following tables:

* The statements of the "International Inquiry Service" no longer correspond to recent recordings. According to Arolsen there were 199 471 prisoners. In the museum the number of prisoners brought to the camp is given as 206 206 as it was recorded by Domagala.

In detail the tables gives the following:

I. Original Numbering			
1933 from	1	to	4 821
1934 from	4 822	to	6 811
1935 from	6 812	to	8 922
1936 from	8 923	to	11 245
1937 from	11 246	to	13 260
1938 from	13 261	to	31 941
1939 from	31 942	to	35 862
1940 from	35 863	to	37 575

II. Second Numbering			
1940 from	1	to	22 985
1941 from	22 986	to	28 980
1942 from	28 981	to	41 564
1943 from	41 565	to	60 869
1944 from	60 870	to	137 244
1945 from	137 245	to	161 944

Goldschmitt *(Western Witnesses)* gives as the last numbering of a prisoner for April 28, 1945: 161 879, but he thinks, however, that 6375 more, being still on the way to Dachau, have to be added, therefore his count for the second numbering is 168 254.

Besides numbers, colours and marks

As the above statistics, arranged according to nationality, of Dachau's prisoners show, there was a variegated mixture of races. This was increased still more by the various political views, social positions, religions, reasons for imprisonment, etc.

In order to enable the camp authorities to recognise at first sight with what type of prisoner they had to deal, individual prisoners had to wear a chevron (a) of certain colours and marks on the jacket and trousers as well as his number.

The red chevron marked the political prisoner,
the green chevron the professional criminal,
the black chevron the work-shy or the asocial,
the violet chevron the Bible inquirer,
the pink chevron the homosexual.

A bar above the chevron indicated that the bearer was already serving a second sentence in the camp (b).

To mark the *nationality*, a corresponding letter was drawn in the cloth angle: F = Frenchman, P = Pole etc. (c and d).

were marked with a particular sign, the Jewish star on a yellow background. The non-Aryans were exposed to special persecution from the beginning of the Third Reich, therefore they peopled Dachau very quickly. On September 22nd and 23rd, 1938, 3800 Jews were brought from Dachau to Buchenwald according to the report of Hans Schwarz. At the same time 5000 light summer uniforms were decorated with the Jewish star, which was a sign that a mass transport of Jews was expected. This did really happen after the attempt Herschel Grynszpan on the life of Dr. Rath, a member of the German Embassy in Paris. The first reaction to it was, as is well known, the *"Crystal Night"* of November 9, 1938, with the destruction of the synagogues, plundering of the Jewish stores, ill-treatment of many Jews, etc. Then the imprisonment followed: 2000 Jews, whose ages ranged from thirteen and a half to eighty-six years, came to Dachau for "Nazi re-education", it was said. Their number increased in fourteen days to more than 13 000 (H. Schwarz). In the following months some of them obtained their freedom when they "voluntarily donated" large possessions to the Reich and promised to emigrate; but, according to Schwarz more than 700 of them died from the severe ill-treatment and privations.

Clergymen in the Dachau concentration camp

The opposition which soon set in by the Christian churches against all the violence, disbelief and immorality of the National Socialism (see my book "Kreuz und Hakenkreuz") brought many clergymen of all denominations, especially many Catholic priests to the concentration camps as well as to the gallows and to the guillotine.

Not less than

2720 Clergymen

came to the concentration camp at Dachau.

They belonged to various nations:

	Total	Released in the course of time	Died in the camp	Transferred to other camps or liquidated	Liberated only in 1945
Germans	447	208	94	100	45
Poles	1780	78	868	4	830
Frenchmen	156	5	10	4	137
Czechs & Slovaks	109	1	24	10	74
Dutchmen	63	10	17	—	36
Belgians	46	1	9	3	33
Italians	28	—	1	1	26
Luxemburgers	16	2	6	—	8
Jugoslavs	50	2	4	6	38
10 other nations	25	7	1	4	13
Total	2720	314	1034	132	1240

According to religion or denomination these 2720 clergymen were:

Catholic	2579	(= 94.88%)
Protestant	109	
Greek Orthodox	22	141
Old Catholic and Mariawits*	8	
Moslems	2	

The Saddest Balance: the number of deaths*

"My life is cut off, as by a weaver" (Is. 38, 12)

Balances should tally.

Whoever will attempt to reach a final reckoning of the number of deaths in Dachau will find that it does not tally. We have already said this in the Introduction.

However, it is our sad duty to say more about this. The "International Inquiry Service" from Arolsen gives the following numbers:

a) died in prison	27 734
b) died after the "liberation" (April 29, 1945)	1 704
	29 438

"To this number an unknown number of prisoners must be added who died before or immediately after the liberation and whose death is not noted in our documents, likewise the number of those persons who died during the evacuation march. (However, we must include thousands of prisoners, especially those in mass transports, who arrived dead in Dachau during the last months, and who were not registered at all.)"

The number of deaths increased in an extraordinary manner for the first time from 1942–1943 when a typical epidemic of typhoid fever swept through the camp at Dachau and a quarantine had to be imposed upon the entire camp for several months. 964 prisoners are said to have been victims of the epidemic at that time.

Annual Harvest by the reaper Death

Domagala gives the following numerical proof of the deaths in Dachau:

	1940	1941	1942	1943	1944	1945
January	—	455	142	205	53	2888
February	17	393	104	221	101	3977
March	86	321	66	139	362	3668

* Mariawits are members of a sect of a polish national church.
* According to the "International Inquiry Service" Arolsen, there were 31 951 certified deaths between 1933 and 1945.

26

	1940	1941	1942	1943	1944	1945
April	101	227	79	112	144	2625
May	87	322	98	83	84	2226
June	54	219	84	55	78	—
July	34	140	173	51	107	—
August	119	104	454	40	225	—
September	134	73	319	45	325	—
October	171	88	207	57	403	—
November	273	110	380	43	997	—
December	439	124	364	49	1915	—
Total	1515	2576	2470	1100	4794	15 384

sum total = 27 8 3 9

It must also be remembered that this numbering of deaths begins only in 1940 and does not include those from 1933 till January 1940.

Father Goldschmitt, introducing this list of the dead, (p. 13) admits:

"Opinions differ widely about the number of prisoners who died in Dachau. The camp office officially stated:

In the years 1940–1945 the number of deaths was:

1940	1 515
1941	2 576
1942	2 470
1943	1 102
1944	4 794
1945	1 719
	14 176

According to the opinion of the prisoners engaged in the office, this number must be trebled. Most of the comrades, in fact, did not die in the camp at Dachau itself, but in transit and in other concentration camps to which they had been transferred."

In reference to these numbers given by Goldschmitt it must be remarked:

a) They do not include the deaths from 1933–1939.

b) In his report on the terrible death rate in the 1945 typhoid epidemic (p. 154) he gives the full figures in place of the official estimate of 1719. He says: "Thanks to the help I received from the offices, I am in a position to give the correct figures for those deaths. The figures were:

27

in the month of	
January, exactly	2 888
February	3 972
March	3 668
April	2 625
The total is	13 153

To this number, another 2 276 must be added. These 2 276 who died after the liberation (April 29, 1945) died as a result of medical experimentations. In all, 15 429 died from typhoid fever in 1945. The number of deaths reported by individual witnesses may vary a little, but all testimony gives evidence of an ocean of sufferings.

"The crematorium could no longer hold all the bodies. In four mass graves the Lothringian Capo of the funeral commando, Schmitt Heinrich, buried 3350 bodies. Dachau's camp offered a picture of horror."

On page 161 he adds:

"On May 15th, the number of sick in Hospital No. 1 was 386, in Hospital No. 2, 3804. Unfortunately, many patients died. From May 1st until 15th, death demanded the life of 1433 comrades."

And yet this is not the full measure of the horror. Many died and were not registered. For example, all who died during transportation came to Dachau only as corpses.

Father Goldschmitt reports it in this way (page 150):

"In the first week of July 1944, two trains arrived with Frenchmen from Compiègne. On July 5th, we experienced something unbelievable. In the cattle wagons, 370 corpses lay among the living. The pen refuses to describe how these pitiable countrymen passed away from hunger, thirst and heat during the journey of several days." – "A German clergyman who was a witness of the transportation of the dead said to me: 'Germany can never make amends for all this!'"

Joos ("Leben auf Widerruf", page 147 ff.) confirms and completes this report as follows:

"The transport of deported French politicians which came from Compiègne on July 5th, 1944 was supposed to bring 2582 men according to the circular list. But only 952 living and 483 dead arrived. The other dead had already been unloaded somewhere on the way. No one in the camp believed the SS who spread the report that the prisoners had fought among themselves on the way and had trampled one another to death. They were suffocated.

Dr. Marsault who served as camp physician in Compiègne was brought to Dachau by force because he refused to mark some sick prisoners as fit for transportation. Later transports deposited their human load as usual on the playground in front of our office windows" (See Chapter 6).

Eighty Children doomed to Death

"Eighty Jewish children were in Dachau for a few weeks. The youngest was eight years old, the oldest fifteen. He felt himself the speaker for all. Unusually mature for his years and already long since well instructed in his trade, he explained objectively to us what he thought of this transportation and of the supposed intentions of the SS-men: 'We shall be killed like our fathers and mothers. We know it. In the camp where we were, some of the group were called every day. They disappeared and we did not hear of them any more. Now it is our turn. They will take us away from here and kick us into the gas chamber. I suppose it must be so' – Fourteen days later it was so" (Joos).

Now we come to the sad story about the

exterminations.

Besides the cases of arbitrary flogging to death and direct murdering of individual prisoners by brutal SS-men, camp-seniors, block-seniors and apartment-seniors and even by the Capos of the infirmary, general massacres and individual executions took place at the order of the Gestapo and the high Nazi leaders. General massacres took place above all in the so-called

Invalids-transports

which had no other purpose than

death by gassing.

As already mentioned, Dachau had, in the last year, also its own gas chamber. But its "showers" were never used. Instead, the inmates of the Dachau camp were sent to Linz in Austria to be gassed. Domagala gives us some details of this for the years 1942–1944:

January	2nd	1942	120	January	19th	1942	100
January	6th	1942	120	January	20th	1942	99
January	9th	1942	120	January	22nd	1942	100
January	12th	1942	120	January	26th	1942	100
January	15th	1942	98	January	27th	1942	100
January	16th	1942	100	February	16th	1942	60

February	17th	1942	100	May	20th	1942	60
February	19th	1942	99	May	28th	1942	119
February	23rd	1942	100	June	11th	1942	29
February	24th	1942	100	August	10th	1942	98
February	26th	1942	99	August	12th	1942	83
March	2nd	1942	100	November	7th	1942	90
March	3rd	1942	97	November	12th	1942	120
May	4th	1942	118	November	14th	1942	120
May	6th	1942	119	December	8th	1942	12
May	18th	1942	116	November	9th	1944	150

Altogether 3166 prisoners were sent to the gas chamber, among them about 700 Poles.

What the gas did not do in Dachau, the bullet did in the same measure in the
general executions.

The number of these victims will never be established. What details we know may really only be a fraction of the whole.

The first general execution, of which precise details are known, took place on November 11, 1940: Fifty-five Poles, former senators, envoys etc. were shot.

In the autumn of 1941, several weeks after the beginning of the war with Russia, mass liquidations took place daily. Well over 6000 were executed, but their names, etc., were not registered.

In May 1944, ninety-two Russian officers were shot – murdered, we must admit.

In the middle of April 1945, I met a Russian general in Dachau. He had been transferred from Flossenbürg. The conversation turned to the execution of the ninety-two Russian officers in May 1944. The general told me that scarcely anything had excited such exasperation nor contributet so much to create the will to resist, which had been absent until then, as the general massacre of Russian prisoners of war in the years 1941/42 and especially the shooting of the ninety-two officers. So abominable as Hitler's crimes were – contrary to the International Law - and so tragic the consequences, the more remarkable was the sentiment which the leading prisoners of all nations in Dachau at that time showed towards their fellow-prisoners doomed to death and especially the heroism and self-sacrifice of the ninety-two officers. As soon as news of the intended execution reached the prisoners' ears, the leaders of the "National Committee" met secretly and unanimously decided that no labour commando would march out if the ninety-two officers were not allowed to accompany them to work. And so it happened. Nobody moved as the command was given to march off to work. The twenty thousand prisoners remained standing silently. The camp leader himself could not explain it and did not receive any answer when he asked the reason. Finally, he sent for the camp clerk and asked him: "What is going on here? Why do they not march off?" The clerk replied: "The camp is angry because of the rumours of shootings which are to take place today."

Then followed a new rigorous order to march off. But still no one moved. This companionable solidarity gripped the ninety-two officers, who werde already separated from the other 20,000 prisoners and stood on the bunker street. No, they do not want to purchase their lives at the cost of endangering 20,000 comrades. So one of them, Tarassow, a lieutenant-colonel stepped forth and called to the prisoners: "Comrades, march off! We shall die as we lived in the struggle for Russia. Good-bye, comrades, march off!" But these do not want to leave their endangered fellow-prisoners. No labour commando makes a move to go. Then the SS-men telephonically demanded two guard companies of 700 men. They came with machine guns and carbines; and still nobody moved. Once again Tarassow stepped forward and cried: "March off, comrades, march off! Good-bye!" And so a third time. As the comrades did not obey the last call, Tarassow asked for a consultation with the camp clerk, himself a prisoner, and emphatically explained to him that they should "blow off". Full of sorrow, the latter made up his mind and gave the catchword: "Comrades, the commandos march off!" They had scarcely pulled off, when fifteen heavily armed SS-men approached, took twelve of the Russian officers into their midst, led them off 1980 feet to the crematorium and, in the range close by, "liquidated" them one after the other. And the fifteen SS-men marched back to the roll-call square to fetch the next twelve; and so they continued until the last had fallen by the bullet. Ninety-two marched silently to death, having rejected the offer of the 20,000 to suffer for their sake.

On February 22nd, 1944, thirty-one prisoners were liquidated near the crematorium and ninety prisoners on September 4th, 1944.

Single Executions

During the entire existence of the camp at Dachau, single executions also took place. Only the rope was good enough for ordinary prisoners. For this reason special poles were erected in the bunker yard. I often looked at these poles in horror, especially when three signs indicated that they were once again in use. The signs were:

Our cells were locked; a motor truck drove into the yard; the "Hausl" (name given to the warder who was a previously convicted prisoner) of the bunker was drunk in the evening; he received a bottle of strong liquor for his "hangman's service" each time.

Two special single executions at the last hour

The first was that of the so-called

"Bürgerbräu" (citizens' brewery) assailant Georg Elser.

A thick veil enveloped him and his outrage. It was characteristic that this joiner journeyman from Munich, who, it was reputed, had made an attempt on the life of the "Führer" (Hitler) on November 9, 1939, was not executed at once as the men of July 20, 1944. He was not even brought to trial, but he was carefully secluded from all the world, first in the camp at Sachsenhausen, later Dachau. Nevertheless, he always enjoyed special privileges, for example, he received a larger cell and a workshop, also sheet music for playing the zither etc. When he was transferred from Sachsenhausen to Dachau because of the approach of the Russians on Berlin, a wall dividing two cells was taken down – men worked all day and night at it – to provide a larger cell for him. However, he was not allowed to come in contact with the other prisoners (except later in the shelter bunker during air raids); a guard had to sit in front of his door continuously. But once I succeeded in getting to him for a short time by deceiving the man on guard during the distribution of gifts. I moved quickly to Elser's door (he had to be called "Eller" in the camp) and said: "There is a new one over there; he should get something too", and I dashed into his cell. In April 1945, he suddenly disappeared. At that time it puzzled us, but it was cleared up, however, when we were transferred to South Tyrol at the end of April 1945. Then our fellow-prisoner Captain S. Paine *Best,* one of the two English officers who had been carried off by force after the Bürgerbräu outrage at Venlo, succeeded in taking an "express letter" from a SS-escort watchman, a letter which the chief of the Security Police and of the Security Service had addressed to the commandant of the Dachau camp on April 5, 1945. This letter, described as "State secret material" contained first, instructions for the treatment of the prisoners, General Colonel Halder, General Thomas, Hjalmar Schacht, Schuschnigg with wife and children and others. Then it continued:

" . . . Also in the case of our special prisoner 'Eller' a conference was held by the highest authorities. The following instructions were issued:

> *On the occasion of one of the next air-riads on Munich or in the vicinity of Dachau, 'Eller' is to be presumed fatally injured.*
>
> *For this reason I ask you to liquidate 'Eller' in an absolutely secret manner after such an occurrence in the camp. I ask you to see to it carefully that only very few persons who are to be bound to secrecy know of it. The notice of the execution to me would then read:*
>
> > *'On . . . , as a result of the terror attack on . . . , the prisoner 'Eller' was among those fatally injured.'*
>
> *Having taken notice of this letter and carried out the instructions mentioned therein, I ask you to destroy it."*

Signature
(illegible)

(See the photostatic copy of this letter in Bests' book "The Venlo Incident", publishers: Hutchinson & Co., London.)

H. Best solved the further riddle for me why they first treated Elser favourably for six years and then suddenly and secretly "liquidated" him by the explanation:

"Very simple. At first they wanted to save Elser for a great staged trial after the victory, in which the 'Intelligence Service' would have been exposed as the instigator of the Bürgerbräu outrage. All the taking of depositions had been practised with Elser. But as they began to realize that the victory would not now take place, the staged trial fell through, the man who hid the secret of the outrage in his breast had to be silenced. An air-raid would give a good opportunity for the 'liquidation'."

Especially tragic was the shooting of the French General

Delestraint

in the very last days of the concentration camp:

Together with Msgr. Piguet, Bishop of Clermont-Ferrand, he was brought from Nazweiler to Dachau in the summer of 1944, "both exhausted and in great pain". (Joos: „Leben auf Widerruf", p. 149.) At the beginning of 1945 both were brought from the general camp to the "bunker" and then transferred in April 1945 as we had been to the "barrack" which the prisoners tenderly called the "girls' high school", but from which the inmates, however, had been transferred, because of the Americans.

On April 19, 1945, the General served the Bishop's Mass. This he had done in an exemplary manner every day since I had succeeded, after energetic protests, in obtaining for the Bishop the right to celebrate Mass in our emergency chapel. During the Holy Mass of that day, an "Untersturmführer" (under-commandant) came in and said: "The General must pack at once." Calmly the General went away, packed his few things and came back to receive Holy Communion. His last Holy Communion!

After Mass I asked the "Untersturmführer": "What is wrong with the General?" – "Ah", he answered lightly, "he is going to Innsbruck, as all of you are. We have just a small bus with eight seats but only seven people. Now we are taking the General with us." Three hours later, Delestraint was shot together with three other French prisoners and eleven Czechoslovakian officers. As Joos "Leben auf Widerruf", page 156) says, he walked towards the wall, naked, his head held high. Before he reached it, two pistol shots had laid him low. He died as a soldier and as a pious Christian.

V. Compulsory Labour

"He set over them masters of the works, to afflicet them wirth burdens" (Exodus, 1, 11).

The slogan „Arbeit macht frei" ("Works makes you free") was, as we have already mentioned, hanging over the entrance to the camp. Here, in reality, work was a means of degrading and enslaving men of all professions.

The kind of work depended on the economic and political situation. During the first years from 1940–1941 work was considered more as a means of training. It took the form of unnecessary digging of the soil and removing it from place to place, of transporting stones or of sifting gravel. And all the time it was not a question of obtaining a result but rather of the amount of pressure which could be exerted on the prisoner while he worked. When work of this kind had to be done, the block leaders and their Capos were always present to see if the wheelbarrows were full enough, if prisoners were standing about idle, smoking, chatting etc. Much work of this kind had to be done at a running pace.

Good opportunities for annoying the prisoners presented themselves in the

rolling of the camp streets.

For the heavy rollers to which under normal conditions at least a couple of strong draught-horses would have been harnessed, ten to sixteen starved prisoners, driven by a row of SS-men and Capos carrying leather whips, were employed. Among the victims were to be found the present Bavarian Minister for Agriculture, Dr. Dr. Alois Hundhammer, as well as the son of the former Prime Minister of Bavaria, Dr. Held. (See picture on the cover page 2.) The lashed and bruised prisoners often fainted from sheer exhaustion and over-strain. Any offence during working hours was punished immediately. Prisoners were struck on the spot and extra work was imposed as a punishment so that the gangs returning from work at dinner- or supper-time often had to wheel some of their utterly exhausted comrades in their barrows and many had to be taken to the infirmary to have their wounds dressed.

Plantation-Work and Torture

In the commando plantation the SS-men executed those who were employed there, especially the Jews, in the years 1940–41 in the following way. They pulled off the prisoners' caps and, having thrown them into the neutral zone, commanded the prisoners to fetch them at once. While they obeyed the command, the SS-men shot them under the pretence that they were trying to escape. In the plantation many priests had to suffer much, indeed, some of them even met their death.

Father Goldschmitt adds:

"Inside and outside the prison camp many gardens were laid out. The largest garden bearing the name plantation was a huge square area under cultivation, approximately 550 yards square. It had been wrested from the Dachauer marshes at the cost of countless human lives. Paths and drains traversed the fertile ground. The plantation was used chiefly for the cultivation of medicinal plants. Jews and priests, hundreds of whom died, had to cultivate the marshy land from 1940–1943. The plantation was, in the truest sense of the word, fertilized with human sweat and blood. During the good weather about 1300 prisoners were employed, in winter between four and eight hundred. The latter cared for the seedlings in the greenhouses, the former planted and looked after countless varieties of tea plants. Vegetables for the inmates of the camp were also cultivated, and even flowers were to be seen though they were used mainly for medicinal purposes. The prisoners cared for approximately 12 acres of swordlilies alone, because of their vitamin content.

In spring and summer the fresh green of the plantation, the smiling flowers and the friendly country houses would have presented an inspiring picture, had it not been for the terrible slavery.

Parish priests were yoked to the ploughs and harrows, and six men apathetically dragged the heavy load along. Carrying water in the drought, collecting tea and drying the tea plants in a temperature of 70° centigrade were very laborious occupations." (Goldschmitt: *Western Witnesses*, page 24.)

Hard work had also to be done in the

gravel pit.

"The gravel pit was considered the worst assignment. At the four corners stood armed SS-rascals. Some dogs specially trained to snap at the prisoners' uniforms ran about barking. The Capo approached with his 'company' – before 1942 they were chiefly priests and Jews. From afar the forced singing of the slaves could be heard. They had barely arrived at the pits before there were cries of: 'Tempo, tempo, you sluts, you filthy Jews!' The hounds barked still louder. It is a hot summer's day, yet at 7 a.m. it is still bearable. Quickly the clothes are thrown into a heap. The gravel commando divides into four groups. Those carrying picks break up the gravel; others shovel it against the wire netting to separate the sand from the rough gravel; a dozen prisoners wheel a heavy wagon forwards. The fourth group throws great shovelfuls of sand or gravel into the wagon. From time to time during the work the shrill cry of the SS-men and the Capo can be heard: 'Tempo, tempo, faster, faster – begin – pick, shovel, fill up, you lazy dogs ... You! come here! You! go there!' Without rest and without peace ... The sun rises higher. Perspiration runs from their foreheads. Blisters appear on the palms of the hands. Fingers are bleeding. Many comrades are suffering terribly from bruises on the thigh caused by the pressing of the shovel against the flesh, and backs are aching from the continuous stooping. Here a prisoner stretches himself and utters a groan, there another rests a little on his shovel. Instantly, the butt of a rifle in the ribs or a kick brings them back to their drudgery. Two hours long this oppressive work must be done, almost without a pause, and all this with empty stomachs. At 12 o'clock, the march begins to the stall where the scanty meal is eaten. On the way, they are forced to sing. At 1 o'clock the race back to the gravel pit." (Goldschmitt, p. 22.)

Even in winter the perspiration ran at the

Snow commando.

"In winter the snow commando was the terror of all those prisoners who had no special duties to fulfil.

Dachau is situated not far from the Alps, almost 1900 feet above sea level. The winter is very severe. Snow often fell heavily from the end of November until April.

The SS would not tolerate snow within the limits of the camp. If the flakes fell during the day, they had to removed immediately from all places and streets. But often at daybreak a quilt of snow one to two feet deep covered the ground. In such cases the snow commando came to the rescue. In the years 1940–1942, the members of this commando were exclusively priests, more than 1000 men strong, young and old. Shovels and boards nailed to wooden planks served to pile the snow in huge heaps. Small barrows and large carts brought the snow to the nearby river Würmbach. If the snow could not all be piled on the carts, it had to be shovelled upon tables which four men carried on their shoulders. The snow commando had to work eight hours daily, always on the go. According to custom, everything was done at a running pace. 'Tempo, tempo!' was heard all day long. SS-hooligans and Capos stood or walked behind the clergy and struck them with sticks. Filthy terms of abuse and double-meaning expressions rained on the poor shovellers. Many an aged parish priest slipped under the heavy load fell to the ground. Even the younger men gasped under the burden of snow piled high on the tables. And lashes and kicks were the rule of the day. The strenuous and unaccustomed work forced the sweat from the pores. Not a few priests lay unconscious on the ground and as a result contracted pneumonia. In the block no one had either clothes to change or an opportunity to dry those which were wet." (Goldschmitt, page 47.)

The dragging and pushing of the

Moor-express

was another degrading, senseless and often painful job. Father Goldschmitt writes (pages 21/22):

"Engines and horses were luxuries for the prisoners. Heavy four-wheeled wagons christened 'Moor-express' served for transport. The prisoners were harnessed to the wagons. The shaft was guided by two men. At each side of the wagon there were three or four wire ropes, with attachments on them called *Koppeln*, each *Koppel* being pulled by two prisoners. Four to six prisoners pushed the wagons from behind. Even though the Moor-express was very heavy, everything had to move at a gallop. An under-Capo usually carrying a stick drove the two-legged "horses" onwards. For transport service outside the camp armed SS-men and dogs accompanied the prisoners. The summer brought heat and dust, the winter snow and mud. With bent backs and lowered heads these human beasts of burden pushed, drew and shoved the Moor-express, eight to ten hours daily, day in, day out, from the camp to the station, from the station to the workshop, from the workshop to the shop, from the gravel pit to the new building, from the kitchen to the barracks and (one could add 'also up to the burial heap, for transporting the corpses') ... It was no longer men who drew the wagons, but machines. Seldom was a prisoner seen to wipe the sweat from his brow, only a few used their handkerchiefs ... All seemed to be full of affliction. In a rage they pressed their teeth together. Their limbs shivered from fatigue and hunger. The flow of speech flagged. For many the moral power of resistance was at an end. Slowly but surely these highly-gifted men who were used as beasts of burden were sinking into the darkest melancholy. Only the thought of God preserved our clergy from the worst. But if it happened that poor Moor-express-pushers possessing no religious stamina committed suicide as a means of escape from this hopeless and unbearable misery, the responsibility fell in the first place on the Nazi tormentors of human beings. My fellow-priest from Luxemburg, Dr. Bernard, was also for a long time one of these Moor-express substitute beasts of burden. In his memoirs he writes: 'My first day at the transport commando "Präzifix": It is March 19, 1941, the feast of St. Joseph – As we push the wagon through the door, I pray to him. My place is on the right side of the wagon and I share the *Koppel* with a young

Polish parish priest from Warsaw. We are the same height and the same weight which is very important when pulling the *Koppel*. He speaks a little French so we can entertain ourselves under the eyes of the Capos and the sentinels. On the smooth street the wagon moves quite easily. But soon our feet begin to ache. From walking bare-footed and from the influence of water they are misshapen and swollen, and as well are not accustomed to carrying heavy boots. When evening comes, we shall have no skin on our feet at all. And yet it is a relief that we do not have to wear clogs where we would have to cramp our toes with each step so as not to lose the wooden boards. It is thawing. The middle of the street is free from snow, but the side "draughthorses" must wade in the slush. We talk little. Each one is absorbed in his own thoughts. Can I hold out? And how much will I get to eat? After an hour we are whistled together. We must go to the station. And what has to be brought to the station? A parcel of screws, as big as two cigar boxes. In our innocence we ask ourselves why eighteen men plus three sentinels plus a five-ton lorry must go to the station. We do not know that prisoners, sentinels and lorry may never separate. That is the supreme principle of all outdoor commandos ... So we draw the heavy wagon with the parcel through the muddy street to the station and back again. Gradually we accustom ourselves to leave off thinking."

Apparently easier, but in reality heavy and dangerous work was

the carrying of the food-containers.

Thrice daily the prisoners had to carry the food in great thermos containers from the camp kitchen to the different barracks. Really a drudgery, especially for beginners, the starved and the weakened.

A clergyman from Luxemburg gives us a vivid picture of this (from Goldschmitt's "God in a Concentration Camp"):

"In the kitchen everything must be done quickly and well, otherwise there are blows! The kitchen is wonderfully equipped. The giant boilers sparkle in their cleanliness ... Before I realise it, I find myself fully stretched on the floor. My comrades help me to my feet before anyone notices. The wet tiles are very slippery for our wooden clogs. I notice how the others do not raise their feet but glide along as one does on a skating-rink. Everything has to be learned.

A long row of boilers divides our group and while we advance we observe anxiously the chalk-written numbers of the blocks for which the containers are intended. Will we be lucky? Block 10, that's not too bad! Up! But the thing can't be raised. It is terribly heavy. I consider myself incapable even of leaving the kitchen. In front of us someone is being trounced. He is one of the newcomers. I note that life is at stake. The others remove their caps and wrap them round the thin, sharp handle and I follow suit. And then off!

The two steps at the exit are dangerous. Once outside, we deposit the containers and hastily change sides. In the same minute someone behind us falls over his own clogs, falls down the steps and the boiling soup is poured over him.

We move in 'contrary motion' so as to avoid spilling the soup and scalding our hands. I am more dead than alive when we finally reach Block 10 with our vontainer."

It was only in 1944 that it was decided to use suitable wagons for transporting the soup.

In the Munition-Factories

As time went on and more workers were needed, the prisoners were also sent to work in the munition-factories. In this way they came into contact with civilians who required that the prisoners be in good working condition. This usually meant better treatment and various facilitations. The most important was that the prisoners were removed from the immediate control of the SS-men. In many cases conditions were not always rosy, because the supervising sentinels and even some of the civilians did not treat the prisoners as human beings, but rather as cheap working power. But, at least, there was not so much capricious and thoughtless beating of the prisoners as had been the case in the years 1940–1941.

Although it still remained forced labour, yet it brought these poor victims outside the camp and into contact with men who were free, many of whom were good and merciful.

VI. „Leben auf Widerruf" – Life by Reprieve

So with Joos we could describe life in the concentration camp at Dachau. Distress and danger were always at hand from the first to the last day. Always the fear of death.

Each prisoner who was brought to the camp had to undergo the process of "admission to the camp". After the particulars had been written and the sectional political officer had compared these with the files submitted by the Gestapo, the prisoner entered the camp where he was received by the camp leader, the report-leader and the whole army of block leaders.

Even on entering the camp abusive language and shouts of derision were to be heard. ("Welcome to Dachau", called a member of the SS mockingly to me as I was committed.) Very often it meant the first boxes on the ears. This I had also experienced in the concentration camp at Sachsenhausen, when I was chased along, up and down, to the other "entrance" and received such a kick from one of the SS-men that I fell to the ground and cut my hands, or while being photographed I was struck in the face with closed fists until I was almost ready to collapse.

The one so welcomed betook himself to the "dressing-room" where all personal belongings had to be deposited. There he was obliged to remove all his clothing, being permitted to keep only a handkerchief or perhaps a belt. Finally he was marched off to the bathroom where his hair was completely shaved off. This work was often done by prisoners who were not professional hairdressers and in many cases the razors were blunt and very painful. After the bath the camp linen was handed out: a drill uniform, trousers and wooden shoes. Attired in this way he was then brought to the office of the camp or barrack where he was given his number. Sever l times he was obliged to give particulars about himself which were written on different lists and card files. Anyone who has never had to undergo such an ordeal can scarcely imagine how degrading all this can be, even more painful than the closed fists which buffetted my face in the concentration camp at Sachsenhausen.

Quarantine

In the beginning, the newcomers were usually assigned to the gravel pit, the plantation etc., on the day after arrival. Later, however, because some arrived sick or there was danger of infection, it was necessary to spend some weeks in quarantine.

During this period of quarantine the prisoner learned the prescribed marching, forms of greeting and reporting as well as German songs and the grades of the SS. Moreover, he attended a so-called "practical course" in order to become acquainted with the obligatory arrangements of the block as well as the camp regulations. A thorough, practical education was given to him by blows and various other forms of punishment like skipping or standing for hours on the street leading to the block, irrespective of rain, frost or heat.

The "theoretical schooling" about life in the camp affected the prisoners more than this ill-treatment of the body. The principal thoughts were: The German society has thrust the newcomer out of its ranks, he has become as it were te expectoration of human society. In the camp he is a mere *number*; he must obey all orders even those given by the lowest grade of the SS; he must observe all regulations exactly; doff his cap before every SS-man and stand still when answering. Escape from the camp was utterly impossible;

the barbed wire fence around the camp was charged with electricity, anyone attempting to escape would be caught again and brought back to the camp.

Letter-writting allowed, but ...

After a definite period the prisoners who found themselves in quarantine were permitted to write letters to their families unless something to the contrary had been expressly decided for them. For these letters special printed notepaper, obtainable in the canteen, had to be used, and all letters had to be written in German. Letters could be written only to one member of one's family and all these were thoroughly censored, some were even destroyed if grammatical errors occurred or if the contents were not clearly formulated. For non-compliance with the regulations in this matter, a penalty was imposed, for example, prohibition of letter-writing.

In the "Convict Company"

Some of the newcomers were assigned to the convict company from the very beginning or came to the camp earmarked "for extermination". Such prisoners were hanged, shot or sent the very next day to the gas chamber in Linz or somewhere else.

Good "Business" – evil means

Some of the block or apartment seniors made use of the naiveté of the newcomers who were not fully acquainted with the conditions of life in the camp to do "business": they stole any utensils which were to be found in the lockers, such as spoons, knives, forks etc., and commanded them to pay for the allegedly lost articles.

On entering the camp all money had to be handed over, but at certain times amounts could be withdrawn for the purchase of cigarettes or other things in the "canteen". The money obtained by doing "business" with "lost" articles was divided among the block seniors. If any one dared to act in a refractory manner or to show displeasure at he business, he was reported at once to the block leader who, by using his clenched fists, brought a knowledge of the camp regulations home to him. On these occasions, the newcomers became familiar with the method of "skipping", with physical exercises when water was often poured over them to introduce variety to the act. Usually after such exercises several of the newcomers remained unconscious, now and then some even lay dead.

After admission to the camp, prisoners were photographed singly; in special cases finger-prints were also taken. I still remember quite clearly how on such occasions the words of Holy Scripture were always in my mind "And with the wicked he was reputed" (Mark, 15, 28).

Daily Routine

Discipline and order ruled with a rod of iron in the main camp at Dachau. The seniors in the camp and blocks had to see to it: report-leaders and block-leaders kept a sharp eye on everything.

Rising-time varied according to the season, mostly between 3 an 5 a. m. Prisoners were wakened early so that all were in good time for the march to the place of employment. Then followed washing, bed-making, tidying the locker and eating breakfast, and all this had to be done in thirty minutes.

After breakfast some prisoners tidied the apartments while the others went to the block street to wait there perhaps half an hour for roll-call, regardless of the weather.

To Roll-Call (even the sick and dead)

Twice a day at 6 or 6.30 in the morning and at 6 p.m. After the morning-roll-call the workers fell into gangs. The evening roll-call sometimes lasted very long especially if the number was not correct straight away. In such a case everyone had to remain standing until the number was rectified or the missing one found again.

January 23, 1939 will remain an unforgettable day for the prisoners who experienced it. It was a snowy winter's night and because two prisoners were missing a thousand others had to stand still the whole night until 11 a. m. the following day on the square, bareheaded; they dared not make the slightest movement to warm themselves. Seven dead bodies had to be carried off the square.

Another nightly roll-call in May of the same year proved even more torturing for the prisoners; they were compelled to stand all night in pouring rain on the square.

Goldschmitt tells us something more:

"We priests were awakened an hour before the other prisoners usually about 3.30 a. m. We assisted at Mass, swallowed coffee and marched in rows of ten silently to the square for roll-call. The same thing took place daily at 7 p. m. Here thousands of men and youths, arranged according to blocks, formed countless rows. The senior of each block commanded: 'Stand still! Caps off!' Then he gave the number present to one of the SS-men who walked up and down the rows checking. The number of inmates in the blocks was then given to a camp leader. We stood here in silence until the officer had ascertained that all prisoners had arrived. If a comrade was missing, which sometimes happened, all had to remain standing until the person concerned was found again. It did happen that the missing one had overslept or had run away. In spite of rain, heat, storm and cold we usually had to wait for a half-hour or perhaps a whole hour. One Sunday we had to stand four full hours in the glaring sun, bareheaded, as the wearing of any type of headdress was forbidden from the beginning of May until September. Many of my comrades collapsed that day. I was an eyewitness when a Polish parish priest, utterly exhausted from the misery of it all, fell dead to the ground. My priest friends told me that shortly before my arrival a roll-call lastet over seven hours. Twenty corpses had to be carried away afterwards. On one such occasion, camp leader R. was on duty. He belonged to that class of dogs which bark much, but don't bite. However, when the fumes of alcohol had gone to his head he would preach 'sermons' which were meant to be funny to us parish priests. Once on a Church holiday, he began with the words: 'Thou art Paul, the rock. Such is your teaching, and it is upon this rock that your church is built.' Some priests spoke up. Now his famous strong language rained on us: 'You dunderheads, you sluts, you motorized wild boars' and the like. At the same time he laughed stupidly as drunkards are wont to do and cried out: 'If he is called Paul or Peter, that's al the same to me. Your Paul-Peter-rock will be blown up, but our rock will remain as hard as steel. We are still at the helm.' R. laid such emphasis on the word 'still' on purpose, well aware that Hitler's rock was about to fall asunder.

'All dead line up for roll-call!' should also have been a command, because until the summer of 1942, all the prisoners who died during the night had to be carried to the square for roll-call in the morning to be counted. The corpses lay uncovered on the ground behind each block. Even seriously ill and crippled prisoners were forced to attend. The healthy carried their weak comrades mostly on their backs or wheeled them in barrows to the square. The German fellow-prisoners turned their embarrassed gaze away from their pitiable companions and we foreigners were filled with rage on witnessing such heartlessness."

A terrible end of a roll-call:

Ten innocent prisoners must die for one who escaped.

It did not happen in Dachau but in Auschwitz; however, it may be added to show under what kind of danger the innocent prisoner lived day by day if one of tens of thousands was missing:

On February 17th, 1941, the Franciscan, Father Maximilian Kolbe, the press apostle of Poland, was imprisoned by the Gestapo (Secret State Police) and soon after brought to Auschwitz. As the escape of a prisoner was noted during the roll-call at the end of July 1941, ten of his living-block had to die and that in a most cruel way, by death from starvation. Among the ten who have been selected without consideration one cried aloud: "Have mercy! I have wife and children." Then Father Maximilian Kolbe stepped forward and offered himself to replace this head of a family and to go with the other nine into the hunger-bunker. The commandant, surprised at such a magnanimity, permitted this exchange. So, Father Maximilian, indeed, went with the other nine in the cell of death and became their comforter and preacher, their leader and example. He endured the terrible sufferings from hunger and exhaustion in full consciousness during two weeks; then they gave him the deadly injection. He died as the last on the evening before the Feast of the Assumption, on August 14th, 1941.

The prisoner No 16 670 was dead but he for whom he sacrificed himself still lives today and thanks him for his sacrifice all his life. God will thank him still more and the Church probably soon will exalt and place him among the holy martyrs.

Peace at last!

The customary roll-call was followed by supper, a wash and preparations for the night rest. At 8.45 p. m. the signal sounded for sleep and at 9 o'clock rest was obligatory. This timetable was often altered in the course of the years. Free time was very limited.

But torturing Suspense

And yet when the prisoner retired for the night, he was not sure what was in store for him the following day. This continual uncertainty was one of the worst things in the camp. The art of survival, if health did not fail, really depended on not being "conspicuous", on not drawing the attention of the leaders to oneself and on not succumbing to a psychical collapse; apart from the fact that a "judgment" of the Gestapo could bring a speedy end. So it was that some never managed to conquer the fear of death.

All kinds of Traps

The prisoners in the convict company had to live under the worst conditions because they were branded as convicts and under this title were conspicuous at every turn. It was difficult not "to be conspicuous" because traps were laid everywhere and at all times for the prisoners. Blows with a stick or other hard object were given on the head if beds were not made properly, the cutlery or utensils badly washed, the "locker" untidy or the soap used up too soon. One had to be on one's guard to escape all complaints, for example, to be in possession of a piece of soap five or six days after distribution: it was really meant for the whole month.

44

It happened that the senior in the apartment on finding a dry towel reproached a prisoner that he had not washed himself and as a punishment slapped him, while it was often an impossibility so reach the wash-room on account of over-crowding. Each wash-room had to serve the inmates of two "apartments". If, as it had been planned, each apartment was to serve forty-five prisoners, then washing would have been possible for everyone and the complaints of the senior would have been justified. As it was there were often more than 300 prisoners in each apartment and so there could be no question of a normal wash. How could one avoid being conspicuous in the matter of washing?

Very special attention was given to the making of beds. In the "locker" the objects had to be put into their respective places. Woe betide him who had any kind of disorder when the rounds were made. His whole locker was painted with coloured chalk, the contents were thrown out. At dinner-time the prisoner was obliged to clean it with sand-paper until all was white, naturally he had to do without his dinner. Those charged with tidying the apartment in the morning could only breathe freely at roll-call, and then only if it were not cold or raining and in Dachau the weather was often bad. The prisoner was very often wet and cold in his prison outfit, and he had just as much to suffer in the hot weather.

The assembling and the march to the square for roll-call took place in such a way that the prisoners formed as it were a guard. The inmates of each block formed into rows of ten and marched off as if on parade. Every one, irrespective of nationality, was compelled to sing German love-songs. It was forbidden to speak or to turn the head during roll-call; when counting was about to start, the command "Caps off!" was given; all had to remain standing still until the block leader had finished checking. Sick prisoners who were not admitted to the sick quarters, were carried by fellow-prisoners to the square and placed at the end to be counted. While working, one had to be on one's guard not to talk or stop for breath. Prisoners returning from work trembled when they thought of what might be awaiting them in the block or apartment on their return if the rounds had been made in their absence.

The rounds were made by the seniors in the apartments and blocks and it often happened that prisoners returning to their blocks discovered that their straw mattresses had been thrown out onto the street. In the meantime they had been searched and finally something had been found which resulted in severe punishment of the offender. In such a way there were ample opportunities for becoming "conspicuous" at every moment and so liable to punishment.

Reported for Punishment and the Result

Blows and finally the report for punishment and extra work threatened every "conspicuousness".

With what did the punishment report end?

The culprit was ordered to appear before the cruel face of the camp leader; before him no explanation or excuse was possible; he dictated a punishment, for example, half an hour at the stake, flogging with a birch or arrest.

At the Stake

Punishment at the stake was carried out in 1940/41 on a spot near the bunker where special posts had been set up, and in later years in the washroom. The punishment (the "tree") took the following form: The hands of the condemned man were put behind his back, fastened with an iron chain around the wrists and then he was hung up on a hook at such a height that the heels did not touch the ground. According to regulation this punishment lasted one hour. It often happened especially if the prisoner had been attempting to collect evidence, that he had to hang two hours or longer and was even beaten by the supervising SS-man.

"Stretched on the Trestle"

Corporal punishment was given in this manner: On the so-called "trestle", the prisoner was tied in such a way that the upper part of the body lay horizontal and the legs dangled over the sides. The SS-men who were oppointed to inflict this chastisement used specially finished *leather whips* which they soaked in water before using, and beat the prisoners on the seat without paying any attention whatever where the strokes fell, so that frequently the kidneys and other parts of the body suffered serious injuries. The usual number of strokes should have been twenty-five, but the number was often greater, sometimes reaching 100. It was a real pleasure for the executioners when the prisoners screamed, cried, sobbed or fainted from pain. I can hear the moans of the prisoners in my ears to this very day. Shortly before punishment was due to start, the delinquent was told that he must count the strokes conscientiously; if, in his great pain, he forgot to do this, the SS-men would declare that they too had lost count and would order him to start counting again.

46

In 1942, Heinrich Himmler ordered that the thrashing of prisoners in all German concentration camps was to be carried out by *inmates* of the camp and not by the SS-block leaders. This was not only a new form of cruelty against the prisoners but a diabolical intrigue! Now, when prisoners died as a result of the thrashing, the leaders could wash their hands in innocence just as Pilate did and exclaim: Not by the SS-men was he whipped to death, but by his own comrades. Of course, the majority of the block seniors refrained from doing this executioner's job against their comrades. Still some were to be found who were willing to do it in order to reap advantages for themselves: professional criminals and their associates formed a special thrashing group.

Solitary Confinement

To the corrective punishment a period of solitary confinement was also added. It lasted from three to forty-two days. A wooden plank bed served as couch. The confinement could be made stricter by *darkening* the cell. The worst punishment of all was the *"standing bunker"*. In a room about the sice of a telephone kiosk (30 × 30 inches) – I still remember well when it was built – the prisoner was compelled to *stand three days and three nights* and was given only bread and water; every fourth night he came into a normal cell, ate prisoners' fare and was allowed to sleep for one night on a plank bed. Then the three days' standing began again. Such were the abominations which the prisoners had to bear from the sadistic Nazis.

In the "standing cell" the clergyman Theissing from Aix-la-chapelle also found himself. He was employed in the sick quarters and during his time there he had made statistical records about the number of deaths resulting from medicinal "experiments" (infection of malaria, suppuration etc.). His courageous and kindly fellow-prisoner *Karls*, the director of the Charities, sent these reports regularly to his office in Elberfeld until the smuggling of such documents was unhappily disvovered. Karls, who thought that the end had come for him, faced the Gestapo investigation officials in all frankness and determination and still came through after several weeks of confinement in darkness. They refrained from "liquidating" him because they feared that his well-concealed material would be published somewhere abroad.

It was not to be wondered at that every prisoner was on his guard not to appear "conspicuous". Immediate death or physical injury did not as a rule follow the corporal punishment; but at the very least wounds which were hard to heal and protracted pains were the usual consequences. More than that, the danger was always present that if one commited the least fault again, more punishments ensued. As soon as an opportunity arose, a "former offender" would be taken to the stake, the trestle or placed in confinement a second or a third time.

Some annoyances and tortures would have been easier to bear had the prisoners been healthy, strong, well-fed and suitably dressed. As it was, the prevailing living, catering and working conditions were of such a nature that a common cold or other slight indispositions was sufficient to result in an incurable disease. This led only too quickly to a physical breakdown, destroyed the self-reliance of good prisoners and made them candidates for the crematorium. Only those prisoners whom one recognised at first glance as being 80% incurable were taken to the infirmary.

Strange Heatlh Precautions

Also associated with these annoyances was the periodical *delousing and disinfecting* of the blocks. This took place often in winter; prisoners had to remove all their clothes, leave them lying and then walk naked through the snow for more than 330 yards to the wash-room where they remained all day. During this time, special devices and means were employed to disinfect the blocks. After the bath the prisoners returned to the block; during this procedure many fell into bad health.

Meagre Rations

One of the most important problems in the camp was the question of ·nourishment for the prisoners. At the time when the Nazis were at the height of their power, plundering the shops of subjugated countries and living on their abundance, men were dying of hunger in the camp. The starving of the prisoners took place so insidiously, so consistently and so systematically that even now one shivers to think of it. On visiting days the menu was altered for the benefit of the prisoners; the consequence was that on the following days food was again economized by giving the prisoners less to eat. This also showed that the SS-authorities took care to conceal even from their own the insufficiency of the prisoners' diet.

"The Machine needs Fuel"

Of course, there were times, especially after the defeat at Stalingrad when a certain improvement in food conditions was noticeable in the camp. But this was not out of love for the prisoners; the object was to make more prisoners available for work in the munition and other factories. To enable them to work satisfactorily, the starved prisoners were given better food to

48

help them regain their strength. In the concentration camp at Dachau skilled workers were retained for the metal and wood-work, all the others were sent off to the different camps. The living conditions for the experts and trained workers were improved by giving them a bonus for difficult work: a second breakfast (Brotzeit) consisting of one-tenth or, sometimes, one eighth of the army bread-ration was allowed them, together with a small piece of sausage.

The food parcels which from November 1942 could be received from home and later also from the International Red Cross in Geneva were valuable and concrete extras for nourishing the starving prisoners in the camp.

The fact that the food for the SS-men also became scarce proved detrimental to the prisoners' share. The former appropriated the supplies which were meant for the prisoners and as a result their allowance was decreased.

Hunger brings out the worst

Mention must be made of the supplying of food to the prisoners who were transported to other camps. In principle, the camp sending off the transport was responsible for the provision of food until the destination was reached. In this sphere atrocious abuses occurred.

The following facts may serve as examples: On November 14, 1942 a transport of prisoners arrived at Dachau from the camp at Stutthof. On arrival one could see corpses of prisoners from which parts had been gnawed, because the leader of the transport, a depraved SS-men, had not allowed any food to be given to the prisoners during the journey. It was the rule rather than the exception that the prisoners got no food during the evacuation transport which sometimes lasted fifteen days. Now, when such prisoners reached the camp, they were exhausted to such a degree that they collapsed on the roll-call square and were incapable of moving.

On reading this shocking report especially the remark about "gnawed corpses of the prisoners" in Domagala's book *Those who went through Dachau*, I was tempted to doubt if such a thing were at all possible even when hunger had driven the prisoners to the verge of insanity. But an eyewitness, Kohlhofer from Munich, confirmed the statement firmly. Moreover, I found a new proof in Joos's book "Leben auf Widerruf", page 147:

"The worst of all which we experienced of such transport was that from Danzig-Stutthof in November 1942. Approximately 900 Polish and Russian prisoners were expected. They were ten days on the way and had food supplies for only two days. On their arrival 300 dead were counted. These had to be shovelled out of the indescribably dirty wagon and six corpses were gnawed; on several parts of the body the bones were bare; this was done not by animals but by famished comrades. Cannibalism in the year 1942 in Central Europe! The survivors passed by us, naked, to the disinfectant bath, a horrible line of ghostly, tottering skeletons, with staring deep-sunk eyes, a dance of death which the fantasy of the painter Holbein could not have equalled. After a few weeks no one remained of the whole transport: other transports from Grossrosen and Mauthausen reminded us of it. 80% of the last transport coming from Grossrosen on February 28, 1945 were corpses" (Joos, page 147).

VII. Christ in the Concentration Camp Dachau

As the statistics in the chapter "The Dachau Concentration Camp: its inmates" show, about 2720 clergymen, among them 2579 Catholic priests, were imprisoned in Dachau. The first German priest to enter the camp in 1940 was Father Franz Seitz, a parish priest from the Palatinate, a district in Western Germany. (Polish clergymen had already arrived in 1939.)

"Scarley had he arrived at the camp when the SS-man pulled a rosary from the priest's pocket and mockingly placed it on his head so that the cross hung over the forehead. Thus he led him up and down the camp, kicking im and striking him with clenched fists, and screaming wildly: 'The first pig from the old Reich has arrived!' Seitz had a picture of Pius XII in his breviary. The SS-man held the picture under the nose of several prisoners and called out: 'The Roman head priest will be locked up in Dachau with all the other priests after the war. Then the Catholic swindle will be finished for ever.' A picture of Our Lady gave this miserable Nazi an opportunity to crack vulgar jokes about the maternity of Mary, blasphemies which no pen dare repeat." (Goldschmitt: "Zeugen des Abendlandes", page 36)

The number of clergymen in the camp increased rapidly. At first they shared the blocks with the other prisoners, but in December 1940 they were given a special block (No. 26). But soon this block was no longer suitable because practically all the priests interned in the camp at Sachsenhausen-Oranienburg were transferred to Dachau, especially many hundreds of Polish clergymen.

The Block Chapel

This assembling of all clergymen in one block for reasons known only to the Gestapo resulted in the erection of an *emergency chapel* for Block 26. The camp authorities were certainly not pleased with this concession "for the priests" but they had to resign themselves to it. On *January 20*, 1941 Holy Mass was celebrated for the first time. Two tables placed together served as an altar. Two sheets, a small standing crucifix, two cheap candlesticks with very tiny candle-ends, a miniature chalice and a missal were placed on the altar. Some 200 priest stood enraptured before the altar while one of their comrades, wearing white vestments, offered up the Holy Sacrifice.

Christ came to His Brothers in the Concentration Camp

"Our poor chapel", writes Father Goldschmitt in "Zeugen des Abendlandes", page 42, "was converted into a worthy house of God as time passed. The imprisoned priests 'organised' an altar with tabernacle, a beautiful figure of Christ, candles, statues and finally even an artistic set of stations. In addition to our simple wooden monstrance we had another one for important feasts. It sparkled like real silver, yet it had been made from empty tin boxes. An Austrian communist prided himself, an quite rightly too, on the fact that he made this monstrance secretly in the workshop under the eyes of the SS-men.

At first only *one* Mass was allowed daily and it was always celebrated by the same priest, a former Polish army chaplain. The priests, all of whom held a small host in their hands, prayed in an undertone with the celebrating priest and at the Communion consumed the Body of their Lord. Solemn Divine Services were forbidden, as was also every form of religious activity outside the chapel. During the day no one was permitted to enter the chapel."

Non-Germans expelled from the Chapel

In October 1941, all non-German clergymen were removed from Block 26 and sent to Block 28 nearby (Poles, Dutch, Luxemburgers, Belgians etc.). A wire fence was placed around the block and a sentry stood on guard. To prevent the non-German priests from even *looking* into the chapel from their nearby block, a thick white paint was spread over the chapel windows. The commanding officer of Block 28 forbade the prisoners all practice of religion and threatened severe penalties for any breach of rule. The prisoners were forced to give up all breviaries, rosaries etc.

Without splendour, but with devotion

From the year 1942, the concelebration of Mass stopped. We communicated as laymen. It was pathetic to see four confrères, clad in thear scanty prison dress and often barefooted, pass from row to row with the ciborium. Every Sunday before roll-call we had an early Mass, and at 8 a. m. a solemn High Mass with sermon. The great feasts of Christmas, Easter, Pentecost and All Saints were celebrated as worthily and as solemnly as in cathedral.

Ordination in the Concentration Camp

"In Dachau we had also an ordination. *Karl Leisner,* a deacon from the diocese of Muenster had been languishing in the camp since the end of 1939. He was suffering from advanced tuberculosis. Often I encouraged him by saying that God would certainly give him the great happiness of being ordained in his native place. Unfortunately, his healty was failing rapidly. In 1944 all hope of a recovery was gone. Yet our loving Saviour was merciful to the deacon. In September 1944, *Msgr. Piquet,* Bishop of Clermont-Ferrand, joined us as a prisoner. Now an illegal correpondence with Cardinal Faulhaber and the Bishop of Muenster began. All the papers necessary for ordination arrived. Episcopal garments and everything necessary for such a ceremony were made by the prisoners in secret. Ring and cross were supplied by the Messerschmitt-works. The Trappist monk, Father Spitzig, made the crozier. The material for the violet soutane and cape was part of the spoils which Nazi thieves had secured for themselves in the Jewish quarter of Warsaw. The English Oblate, Father Durand, provided a silk mitre decorated with pearls. Cardinal Faulhaber sent us the necessary oil and the ritual from Munich. Everything was arranged so carefully and so secretly that only a few priests in our block knew about it. Not one of the Nazis suspected anything, neither the preparations nor the ceremony itself.

On December 18, 1944 the young deacon, a slim figure with feverglowing cheeks, stood in our apartment, No. 2. The Bishop put on the episcopal garments over his prison dress. Alas, everything was so poor and yet it suited our milieu. The procession to the nearby chapel commenced. All the seminarians and even many laymen as well as the former Capos and fellow-prisoners of his commando were permitted to attend the touching ceremony in the chapel. As there was not enough room for all, we priests remained outside, silently following the sacred action.

After some days the newly-ordained priest had regained his strength and was able to celebrate his first Mass on December 26, 1944. On this, the greatest day of his life, he stood at the altar, far from his mother and father, his brothers and sisters and his friends. He wept and we wept with him. Silently, behind locked doors, we took some photographs of this first Mass so that the parents could see at least the picture of their son celebrating his first Mass in the concentration camp at Dachau.

The young priest, Karl Leisner, never saw his home again. He died a few weeks after the liberation in a sanatorium near Munich.

As in the days of the Catacombs

The Polish priests, as we mentioned earlier, were not permitted to practise their religion in the block so they had to devise means to help themselves. They asked the Capo in charge of the chapel, a priest from Block 26, to give them hosts and wine. Many Polish priests worked in the plantation green-houses. While one of them kept guard and the other comrades pretended to be working, the Polish priest who had spent the longest time in the camp knelt on the ground, with his face turned towards the greenhouse so as to give the impression that he was weeding. Indeed, the SS-sentries might be spying from their watch-tower. The kneeling priest had pressed a small portable altar into the ground and there he celebrated Mass. Many comrades hurried by, holding grass or plants in their hands as if they had some work to do there. They also knelt down and received Holy Communion from their own hands. The Poles were never caught when performing this holy action in these modern catacombs.

From 1941 until 1943 the SS-guards in the block for Polish priests saw to it that only great haters of religion were employed as personnel there. Hence there could be no question of Mass inside the block. After the defeat at Stalingrad, however, Polish priests replaced the block- and apartment-seniors. Now, without candles and without vestments, a priest celebrated Mass in each apartment daily before roll-call. Polish laymen also attended the Mass. Msgr. Piquet, wearing only a stole over his prison dress, celebrated his first Mass secretly in the Polish block.

At the International Eucharistic Congresses amid the cheers of a jubilant Catholic people, Our Saviour, enthroned in a golden monstrance, celebrates His triumphs. But as often as priests and laity walked quietly through the camp street at Dachau holding the Sacred Host in a piece of paper, the glory given to Christ was greater and the joy of the poor prisoners was more ardent than that of the pilgrims attending the powerful Eucharistic demonstrations. A French commandant d'Etat Major once reminded us of the great words of Pascal: "L'homme n'est grand qu'à genoux devant Dieu." "Man is only great on his knees before God." Yes, many comrades in Dachau felt that man can only feel himself strong when he kneels before God.

(From "Zeugen des Abendlandes" by Father Goldschmitt, page 50):

God's Commandment is above SS-Orders

The priest prisoners used every opportunity to care for the religious welfare of their comrades. Of course, they had to be very careful because on the one hand, as we already stated, religious activity was forbidden and on the other there was always the danger of betrayal.

I had to experience this personally. A former Italian minister had arrived in the bunker. On the morning after his arrival he asked me quickly in passing to give him General Absolution, and after a few days he requested me to hear his confession. When the corridor was empty, I slipped into his cell and complied with his wish. We had just finished when the "Hausl" of the prison, a Bible inquirer, entered the cell. Guessing what had taken place, he betrayed me – in spite of all the favours which I had rendered to him in the course of our imprisonment. The hatred against confession was greater than the gratitude for favours. As a punishment I had to remain indoors for a whole week.

The priests in the main camp had the greatest opportunities for caring for the spiritual welfare of the prisoners in the infirmary, and even better chances came after 1943 because from then on, clergymen were employed as nurses there.

"Of course, they were also concerned about the immortal souls of those prisoners who asked for spiritual aid. Twice when outbreaks of typhus raged, many priests volunteered as nurses in the fever hospital. Four colleagues contracted the disease and died there.

The above-mentioned Father Fritz Seitz from the Palatinate had been appointed porter in the hospital in the year 1943. In the early morning he used to sneak into the chapel, take some consecrated Hosts from the tabernacle, hide them in a corner of his underclothing and bring them to the dying. Later, when all priests were driven from the hospital, individual priests, aided by Catholic doctors, themselves prisoners, contrived to bring consolation to the sick. If this was not possible, we gave the Holy Communion to the lay nurses, the personnel and the doctors. The sacred species were given to the patients and they communicated themselves. Our compatriots, Lucien Untereiner from Metz in Lorraine, and many other laymen administered Holy Communion to the sick, and also to those in good health. A very special and holy zeal was shown by the present Minister of Justice, Edmond *Michelet*. He often brought the Sacred Host to Bishop Msgr. Piguet in hospital, and in other cases played the part of Tarcisius. A sick comrade broke a small piece of glass in the wash-room window and removed it. I myself sneaked along carefully and through the opening handed him a cigarette packet containing Hosts for the dying and the healthy.

In 1945, Father Pereira, S.J., published an article in the Paulinusblatt entitled *Christ in Dachau* from which the following is an excerpt:

'Priests' volunteered for service in the infirmary as nurses or warders and did the dirtiest and meanest work there just to be near the dying. The Holy Oil and sometimes the Sacred Hosts were brought to the infirmary by comrades from Block 26, unofficially, of course, and in secret. Here the Polish and French priests deserve special mention. The unselfish love they showed for their fellow-countrymen often resulted in the sacrifice of their own lives. Such was also true of the German priests who gave their lives for their brothers. Many a layman was privileged to play the role of Tarcisius in bringing Holy Communion to the sick when it was not possible to send a priest to some cells. And here hundred passed blissfully to their eternal reward . . .'

We priests also heard the confessions of the healthy prisoners when requested to do so, and gave them Holy Communion in a paper, in a white cloth or in a small box. Priests often distributed Holy Communion on the roll-call square in time of darkness when the SS-people were counting the other blocks." (Goldschmitt, as above.)

VIII. Lights in the Dark

Mutual suffering reconciles and unites

Much terror and sadness have been reported in the concentration camp at Dachau. But, even there, "some little lights shone in the darkness", there were some consolations and some words of encouragement; much opposition was overcome, a spirit of helpfulness was awakened and some true and lasting friendships were made.

How beautiful is the testimony which Father Goldschmitt gave about a communist:

"Our apartment senior, *Willy Bader,* ruled in Apartments 3 and 4 like a good papa. The small, broad-shouldered man with the languished, pale features looked serious and sorrowful. Willy had forgotten how to laugh heartily. No wonder! We newcomers looked with respect, yes, with a certain horror upon his number, the lowest one which met my gaze, No. 9. Since 1933 this brave man had languished behind the barbed wire of Dachau. The poor wretch's experiences must have been terrible, to have made him so misanthropic and taciturn. In spite of our different political and religious views, a true and sincere friendship united me with this communist for thirty months. A hard word never cressed his lips; he never ill-treated one of his fellow-sufferers and, whenever possible, he always gave a helping hand. If we had only had men like Willy Bader als block personnel and Capos in Dachau, then thousands of comrades would have survived. In his loving kindness Willy Bader went so far as to help us priests to bring the Sacraments to the dying in spite of warnings of severe punishment. Unfortunately, this thoroughly honest man died before the liberation."

Joos ("Leben auf Widerruf") dedicates the following tribute to this communist: "The most interesting man among the communistic prisoners was probably Willy *Bader,* a transport worker from Ludwigsburg, who was the senior of the entrance block in 1943/44. He could say of himself that he bore one of the first numbers of the camp Dachau above his chevron, namely No 9. This man was the personification of justice and conscientiousness. He stated quite naturally: 'I ask myself every night if I did wrong to one of my companions in the apartment today'. He died in March 1945 from an attack of hunger typhoid. His comrades laid the first spring flowers on the coffin which those in charge of the mortuary had prepared for him; and there were many, very many, even priests, who mourned for him."

Our apartment senior *Kopp* was a solicitor from Frankfurt on the Main. He was a middle sized man, forty years old, stout, with an intelligent look, an appearance commanding authority and a winning facial expression. He was always polite to all his fellow-sufferers. Only those who stole from their companions felt his hard hand. When his work brought him into contact with the SS-men, he played the smart diplomat. This tactful solicitor kept his apartment in perfect order and all decent prisoners were very attached to him. Wherever help was needed, he was there. I chatted to him for long periods. As a loyal Catholic he gladly joined us priests, without offending the convictions of ohter fellow-prisoners. Kopp understood perfectly how to brighten up some very sorrowful hours during our painful stay of four weeks in the barred block, No. 15. He was discharged in the year 1943 to serve with the armed forces.

Our block secretary, a Czech, a teacher by profession, was also a very good friend in need to us newcomers.

Comrade *Schremmer* still remains vivid in our memory. He was in charge of our canteen and being a teacher had to conduct our so-called re-schooling at that time. Nothing could disturb the equanimity of this tall man with the pale face and friendly eyes. Hundreds of questions were put to him. Everybody wanted to know how it was in the camp, to which work one would be appointed, if Dachau was as bad as reported and the like. A friendly answer was always forthcoming. When some alarming news was whispered from ear to ear, Schremmer scarcely permitted himself a wry smile and always remarked drily: Children, don't get excited! Do not believe anything. These are just lavatory jokes." Schremmer belonged to the highly educated class; he was a director of *Munich's Theatinerverlag* and had come behind the barbed wire because of his loyalty to Church and king. Often he brought Holy Communion secretly to his companions.

Besides these comrades who belonged to the staff, I soon made good friends also among the newcomers. The sixty-nine year-old priest, Father Cordonnier, a Belgian, was very dear to me. This stout old man, who bore his years well, had already spent some months in various prisons. Many ulcers resulting from hunger plagued him. On his arrival in Dachau he was pushed from the truck by the SS-men and broke his nose. The short-sighted man lost his glasses at that time and could no longer read, a misfortune which he regretted very much. His face was also deeply scarred. This fine former professor at the seminary of Liège brought his talents as teacher into the camp at Dachau. How often did he utter words of enlightenment, intercession and sometimes even of reprimand. Among the comrades were plenty of good-fornothings with green and black chevrons, lazy fellows, drunkards, even criminals. One man would ridicule the priests, another would tell dirty jokes, another steal bread, soap and other articles from his companions. Among us there were barbarians, unmannerly louts, braggarts, gossips, know-alls, brawlers of all shorts. Father Cordonnier who spoke German quite well tried to mediate between the quarrelling cocks especially during the absence of the apartment senior Kopp. Full of courage and energy he attacked those who ridiculed the priests and mocked at religion and often he silenced them" (Page 69 ff.).

Michelet also reports similar examples ("Rue de la liberté", p. 203 ff.) of the

> *Spirit of comradeship and readiness to help*
> *Generosity and magnaminity*

to be found in the camp.

A physician offers himself

Michelet reports that Dr. Marsault became a legendary figure in the camp. Everybody knew that he had come to Dachau as it were voluntarily. He had directed the hospital of the camp at Compiègne for a long period of time.

One day he refused to sanction the transfer of a sick person whom he considered unfit for transportation. Hearing this the SS-man addressed him angrily: *"Well then, you take his place!"* And Marsault went – to the concentration camp at Dachau and offered his services to the sick in a spirit of self-sacrifice. (Marsault is the present president of the "International Dachau-Committee".)

Generous Renunciation

Camill Blaisot, the former deputy from Caen, was also among the French prisoners. As he suffered extremely from the cold winter of 1944/45 his great desire was to get warm underwear. His friends did their best to "organize" a woollen jacket for him. After several unsuccessful attempts, they finally succeeded. Triumphantly they brought the pullover to Blaisot. And Blaisot was overjoyed when he saw the long desired garment. But as he looked around and could read sadness, even envy in the faces of some of his companions, he said: "Give it rather to him over there. He is seventy-two years old, I am just sixty-eight."

The locksmith-master Emmerich Hornick told me the following: "At the end of 1944, I told our fellow-prisoner Father Friedrichs, chaplain to the police, in Block 26 that the sick in the infirmary were suffering terribly from thirst and that in the canteen between 30,000 and 40,000 bottles of mineral water were stored, but that the sick had no money to buy a drink. Father Friedrichs replied at once: 'Then Block 26 will see to the payment.' He went back to his block immediately and told his priest comrades about the conversation he had had with me, and the collection began at once. That very same evening he was able to hand over two thirds of the required sum to me and the balance on the following day."

When the Allied forces began to approach from the neighbouring countries and even from different parts of Germany and the food parcels which the prisoners were accustomed to receive no longer arrived, the priests did without their camp bread in order to give it to those who could no longer receive parcels.

The assistant nurses of the blocks were

self-sacrificing even unto death.

Prisoners had often spoken with contempt of the block nurses, but when the need came their work for the sick was heroic. They worked without the help of medicines, with no remedies whatever, with no possibility of

58

immunising themselves against disease. They took the sick in their arms, helped them to turn over, worked indefatigably, even to the point of imprudence. Once, in the space of a few days, death snatched thirteen of them.

Service rendered to the dying and the dead

Michelet humbly tells of himself:

"I was a night nurse for some time in the infirmary. This was not a bad occupation, in comparison with many others it was just enviable. Naturally, one could not close one's eyes or dream, one had to be always ready to follow the call of a patient who sighed: 'Water', or to put others in order again who had dirtied themselves and then to clean the straw mattress too; finally the corpses had to be provided with a label (a piece of cardboard bearing the prisoner's number which was bound to the toe) and brought to the mortuary. This was an exhausting work, particularly as the number of dead increased daily to ten, even twelve to fifteen. The dead bodies had always to be carried through the corridors to a room where an empty place could be found. Moreover, the corpse had to be placed on top of the heap of bodies and sometimes it fell down again . . ." (Page 225).

The archcommunist at Mass daily – for his friend

While rendering service to the typhoid stricken, Michelet himself contracted the dangerous disease. In front of the chapel door he lay unconscious in the snow. His friends carried him to the infirmary on their shoulders. Among the nurses who attended him was *Auboiroux*, a convinced communist, with whom Michelet had brushed all the door latches with disinfectant twice daily for weeks.

When, after weeks of suffering, the crisis was over, and Michelet had regained consciousness, *Auboiroux* asked him if he could do him a favour. Michelet could think of nothing special; he was still rather apathetic. Then Auboiroux said: "Ah, I know what troubles you. You cannot go to the chapel every morning. Well! I will go for you until you are fit to go again." And so it happened that the priests of Block 26 were greatly surprised to see Auboiroux, the well-known French communist of the disinfectant commando, keeping watch for a friend before the tabernacle on the following days. He was wearing his cloak, a short white one which, however, had already become yellow, his pockets filled with his healing charcoal pieces, the pail of disinfectant at his feet. (Michelet "Rue de la liberté", page 203.)

Volunteers in the midst of infection

Like Michelet, many other prisoners volunteered courageously to nurse their very ill comrades, among them twenty Catholic priests (ten from Block 26, Germans, and ten from Block 28, foreigners).

In his book "Leben auf Widerruf" (page 156), Joos dedicates the following tribute to his friend Michelet:

Fully aware of the danger, Edmond Michelet, author of the book *Rue de la liberté - Dachau 1943-1945* (Publication Du Seuil, Paris), now the French Minister of Justice, volunteered for service in the disinfection "death commando".

He wanted to do something special for his comrades. After a few weeks he had succumbed to spotted fever. He was one of the few who recovered, who came to life after several days of feverish darkness. He recovered quickly and then is fell to his duty to hand over his sick comrades to the care of the occupying Allied troops. He persevered faithfully at his comrades' side and was one of the last to set out on the journey to his home country. Before he left, he founded the *Amicale des Anciens de Dachau,* as a token of mutual help in future need.

"No real devils"

Prince Alois of Loewenstein who was President of the Central Committee of German Catholics for many years once said something to me about which I was often to think during my life: *"There are few men who are real angels, but there are still fewer who are real devils.* In every man, even in the most depraved, some goods is hidden. It is our duty to find this good and to help to develop it." I was often to experience the truth of these words during the years of my imprisonment in the concentration camp at Dachau, especially on the first Christmas which I spent in the bunker of the camp. First came the great surprise: The Gestapo permitted me to receive the requisites for the celebration of Mass which His Eminence, Cardinal Dr. Michael Faulhaber had kindly sent to me; the camp administration allowed us to have a temporary chapel in one of the cells; after 322 days without Mass I was able to celebrate the Holy Sacrifice for the first time on Christmas Eve 1941. Moreover, the guards of the bunker (the camp prison) permitted a fellow-prisoner Dr. Michael Höck and me to play "Santa Claus". We distributed the gifts which we had received to all the prisoners. Yes, the guards even brought us a fir tree which we placed in the 300 feet long corridor and decorated as a real Christmas tree. And finally, the "Essklappen" of all the cells (opening through which food was given) were left open for a few hours. This concession enabled the prisoners, some of whom were sentenced to death, to hear the Christmas hymns and carols which we sang in the corridor. So it happened that we could bring the Christmas message and the joy of the Holy Season to all "our brothers in chains" who were deprived of their Christmas Mass. The same great joy was ours on each of the three following years when we had to spend the feast of Christmas in the prison of the concentration camp at Dachau.

IX. Golgotha

Still higher to the mount of suffering even though the walk may be difficult. There we see our fellow-men and we involuntarily want to cry out with compassion and horror: "Ecce homo!". Men who were perfectly healthy, but who were tortured and oppressed out of avarice and desire for murder, degraded and misused as guinea pigs, heartlessly left to die in masses.

The infirmary becomes a place of horror

One is strangely affected to see Dr. Sales Hess describe the infirmary at Dachau as the first of three abodes of horror (Dachau – a World without God, p. 175 ff.). One would expect to find pain and sickness in an infirmary, granted, but one would also expect to find there charity, careful nursing, soothing and healing. In Dachau, however, the infirmary was a "place of horror" which everybody avoided who was not afflicted with a serious illness.

Gold Teeth a danger to Life

A patient who complained much or who did not follow all the orders of the nurses – they knew very little about medicine and nursing in any case – ceased to suffer very quickly. He received an injection which soothed all pains – by taking away his life. But of what value was the life of a prisoner to the SS-physicians or to the nurses – themselves prisoners. Father Seitz who became a nurse at the end of 1942 tells in his sermon *A breach of the Truth* (page 6): "Among the nurses two, especially, were notorious for their sadism and barbarity. By using injections, they caused the deaths of countless prisoners." Another prisoner told me that deadly silence reigned in the sick quarters when these two went from bed to bed with the injection-basket on their arm.

Woe to him who arrived in the infirmary with gold teeth! His sickness was serious and incurable in any case. An injection hastened his death. The SS-physician and the nurses divided the gold teeth . . .

Barbaric Experiments

Medical science was enriched in this infernal world in new ways. Certainly, it is praiseworthy when physicians undertake experimental tests to find out how the human body reacts to this and that new medicine. But every physician, conscious of his responsibility, takes care that his subject will not suffer any injury. Such a consideration, however, did not prevail in Dachau.

Experiments with Malaria

"A physician, Dr. Klaus Sch. (sentenced to death by the Allied court), wanted to test a remedy for malaria. Malaria, a tropical disease, did not prevail in Dachau. He could have gone to the tropics to make his tests there. But why go to such trouble? One could make everything more convenient in the concentration camp. He had the mosquitoes imported from the southern countries, had 300 prisoners assigned to him, later he misused still more, well over 1000; he let the insects bite them and so he had his patients. Well, he first *made* his patients, but he *could not heal them*. Most of them went about with malaria during the entire duration of the imprisonment, always tormented by fresh attacks, and many of them still suffer to the present day. Countless priests were among the victims, particularly Polish, but also German."

Experiments with Ulceration

"Another physician wanted to test a remedy for that purulent inflammation of the membranes which in German is called Phlegmone, and which was common in Dachau. It was usually cured by traditional remedies in the infirmary if it was not too far advanced. But this physician wanted to test a new biochemical remedy. However, instead of choosing people already suffering from the disease, he selected twenty healthy priests and induced the disease in them. I recently had the opportunity to see the original photographs of this experiment. Purulent wounds as big as the palm of my hand covered the feet, legs and arms. Of these twenty priests twelve died as a result of the test. Only eight survived after excruciating torments. Some of them had to have arms and legs amputated. No one called the physician to account. Everything was all right."

Experiments with Temperature

A full series of experiments were made, on behalf of the German Air Force, by Dr. R. (shot by the SS-men themselves at the end of April 1945). High pressure, low pressure, high temperatures, low temperatures etc. A comrade who was later employed with me in the plantation told me the following: Once he had to lie naked upon a table the whole night through in the cold season with the windows open. Soon he faited, but his heart kept beating. He held out till the morning. If his heart had stopped beating then, it would have meant one prisoner less, nothing more.

On other subjects the temperature of the body was artificially lowered to 27° Centigrade by using water and ice. Every ten minutes the assistants had to take the temperatures and mark them in curves. Most of the curves ended somewhere with a cross, and on the margin the off-hand remark "At this temperature the experimental object died" could be read.

This was reported by Father Karl Schmidt who had to photograph the curves. Hundreds of men lost their lives during these experimental tests, suffering every possible torture.

The Devil's Book-keeping

During the war the prisoners were hired out and full use was made of them for the armaments industry, under a strong guard. In the office of the Dachau concentration camp an official estimate of the profit thus to be made was discovered. It read as follows

Average daily amount for loan of prisoner	RM 6.—
Deduction for food	RM —.60
Deduction for use of clothes	RM —.10

Average duration of life: 9 months
$$= 270 \text{ times RM } 5.30 = \text{RM } 1431.—$$

Proceeds from rational disposal of the corpse:
1. Tooth-gold, 2. Clothes, 3. Valuables, 4. Money

Deduction of the costs for cremation	RM 2.—
Average net profit	RM 200.—
Total profit after 9 months	RM 1631.—

Plus proceeds from the utilization of bones and ashes.

"Hippocrates, cover thy head before such brutality!", one might cry out in horror.

X. The end of the Dachau camp is near, but also that of thousands of its inmates

Already in 1943/44 a wave of abdominal typhus had swept over the camp at Dachau and taken away some hundreds of lives. But what was this in comparison to the plague which a year later this

monster from the Orient and the Balkans

spread in the entire camp for months. Let us give the word again to one who was an eyewitness of all the sufferings of the dying, whose heart bled, whose lips tell the truth, the absolutely trustworthy *Joseph Joos* ("Leben auf Widerruf", page 152):

"The frantic mass transports from the Balkans continued. Concentration camps were being evacuated head over heels in the East, South and West. All to Dachau! How would it end? Overnight the blocks were overcrowded threefold, fourfold, sixfold. The masses were jammed into the barracks and in the narrow block alleys. Rest and sleep were out of the question. And vermin were everywhere.

On the day when Jacob *Koch,* the unfortunate Capo responsible for the disinfection of the camp, breathlessly shouted to us: 'Come and see! Millions and millions of insects! The clothes which the newly-arrived prisoners have discarded are moving!' And afterwards in a subdued and oppressed tone: 'I don't believe we can control it any longer. We shall all perish.' – Then we knew enough.

Jacob gave the medical superintendent no peace. Report followed report. 'Mr. Superintendent, it's impossible to go on. The quarantine is useless. We do not have sufficient disinfectants and the blocks are full of lice. Too many men. We cannot move ourselves any more.' The medical superintendent had heard it, yet nothing was done. Days and weeks passed. Hundreds were already raving in fever. Men who had been wholly healthy up to now – Dachau old-stagers, valuable block-personnel – were wiped out in a few days. When it was too late, foolish, precipitate measures were adopted which, instead of saving lives, hastened the disaster.

What took place in the camp at Dachau from the end of 1944 and during January and February 1945 belongs to the most staggering tragedies in the history of all concentration camps. Here, the testimony of survivors from the block of the old and sick prisoners, especially that of thirty-one years-old war invalid *Paul Ferrier* who wrote while the impression of these terrible experiences was still fresh in his mind:

Four distinguished guests, former prisoners (left to right): Fritz Schäffer, German Minister of Justice; E. Michelet, French Minister of Justice; Prince Xavier Bourbon; DDr. A. Hundhammer, Minister of Agriculture. – Photo: Tögel

* * *

Preceding page: The Auxiliary Bishop of Munich, Dr. Johannes Neuhäusler, who himself was imprisoned at Dachau for four years, dedicates the chapel to the Agony of Christ (the monument of atonement) on August 5th, 1960. – Photo: Pospesch

'We were full of lice and fleas. Many had no longer a mattress and lay upon the boards naked. As they could not get up, they had to comply with the needs of nature on the spot. From the upper beds, the excrement fell on those below. If a prisoner was very dirty, he was dragged into the washroom at the comrades' request, the dirt was scrubbed off with rough brushes and then he was thrown upon the boards again. Camille, the Controlleur général de l'armée died soon afterwards. The fisherman, Michel Schulz, forty-four years of age, remained three weeks naked upon the boards without receiving any treatment. Believed to be dead, he was thrown upon the heap of corpses. Using every effort of his will, he succeeded in reaching his bed again. On January 5th, 1945 we had to go back from the bath to the block (about 1320 feet) in intense cold, dressed only in short drawers and a thin shirt. Some collapsed on the way and died (Davier from Nantes). *We were without clothes and blankets for three days.* When these were brought back from the disinfestation, they were still full of vermin. On account of this disinfestation Cherpittel from Belfort, sixty-three years old, received terrible floggings on the head from the block senior Zepp (probably Sepp, the author) and died a few hours later.

The disinfection of January 25, 1945: We had to go to the bath at *6 a. m.* Anyone who could not walk was thrown naked or half-naked upon a wheelbarrow. It was bitterly cold. Many of us had temperatures of fourty degrees (Centigrade). He who did not get along quickly enough received floggings from the block senior, and anyone who did not succeed in reaching the shower at once was pulled along the cement floor and plunged into a water tank. The prisoners de Maudhuy and Durfour were drowned. The Capo in charge of the bath took part in this maltreatment. *On this one day alone seventy-four comrades out of 350 in our apartment died.* The return to the block took place at *8 o'clock in the evening, barefooted*, and many were without clothes. Accordingly, we had been kept in the bath for fourteen hours without food or drink. In the following days the number of deaths increased quite considerably. The corpses with an identification card on the toe (a piece of cardboard on which the prisoner's number was written) were piled up in tens in the washroom and along the baracks. From there they were brought to the crematorium after the gold teeth and the fillings had been removed. Such a life continued in Block 30, especially in Apartments 3 and 4 until the Allies arrived. In Block 30, the block senior, the apartment senior and the door guard were always armed with sticks. Without the brutality and with a little more charity, some of our comrades would certainly have survived!"

65

"Walking Corpses"

"We are writing on Saturday, April 28, 1945. A long procession of newcomers passes through the gate. They are mostly walking corpses. Some fall down dead. The political bureau does not distribute numbers any more, it learns, however, from the accompanying lists that there are 116 women from Leipzig, many of whom are very sick, and 5628 men from seven other camps. Above on the dead tracks of the camp are fifteen to twenty wagons containing 2600 corpses. They are mostly comrades from Flossenbürg and Buchenwald who died of hunger in the wagons. The funeral-commando transports the bodies to the crematorium. The gruesome work lasts until midnight. Mountains of bodies are piled up high at the depot on the railroad, at the crematorium and on the block street of the infirmary. I have many photographs of these pictures of horror in my possession." (Goldschmitt: "Zeugen des Abendlandes", page 158.)

And that on the day before the liberation!

The last terrible days

On April 27, 28 and 29, 1945 one experienced a frightful agitation in the camp because the shots of the artillery and of the machine-guns came closer and closer. The American planes flying very low over the camp and destroying the leading approaches and other important military objects gave us great hope in those days of uncertainty and expectation.

On April 28, 1945 news went through the camp that the entire camp together with its inmates was to be destroyed during the night by order of Himmler. This news almost drove the prisoners mad. However, this plan was not executed. It is supposed that the former camp commandant Weiss, at this time inspector of all concentration camps, prevented the order from being carried out. Further facts on this are not known.

The gate opens to freedom: April 29, 1945

And to the great joy of the entire camp the liberation by the American soldiers began.

Before that, the single watch-towers, one after the other, had hung out white flags, a sign for capitulation. The commandant of the guard-unit demanded the day's report from the officer leader and prepared the capitulation and the formal surrender of the camp to the approaching American army.

At that time the American soldiers had not intended to occupy the territory upon which the camp Dachau was located. An advance party of a small group had come to the railroad depot in the vicinity of the camp and found there a great number of dead bodies in the wagons. Without having a clear idea of where they were going, they advanced further and not finding any resistance, they suddenly found themselves in the camp. The sentries in one of the watch-towers who did not want to surrender were liquidated.

After the entry of the small American advance party, an immense joy filled the hearts of the prisoners. All went to the roll-call square which still held such terrible memoires for them and thanked the liberators.

Soon the flags of various countries were unfolded from the living quarters and from the former administration buildings. The papal flag flew from the priests' barrack. In the chapel the Te Deum was sung. An altar was erected outside the priests' block and Holy Mass was publicly celebrated. During the night, comrades erected a huge cross on the roll-call square. The sacrifice of the Mass was offered on the following day for all the deceased.

And then came the great farewell and the return to freedom and homeland, to family and profession.

XI. A worth monument

To the honourable memory of the victims,
for the atonement of the crimes,
as a lesson for all visitors to the camp
for the peace of all nations.

Already at the end of July 1945, two months after the end of the war,

Cardinal Dr. Michael Faulhaber

wanted to erect a monument to the memory of the victims of the concentration camp at Dachau and also a monument of atonement for the crimes committed there.

With this in view, he wrote to General Dwight Eisenhower, at that time the commander-in-chief of the Allied Forces in Europe.

Immediately, the camp was in use again for the imprisonment of the former leading Nazis, SS-men, etc., and this led to the construction of an emergency church which the prisoners themselves, under the initiative of Father Leonhard Roth, curate, erected in 1945. (Later a Protestant church was also erected.)

The International Committee of former prisoners of the camp at Dachau called "Comité International de Dachau" with its headquarters in Brussels passed a resolution to erect a monument on the former roll-call square of the camp and for this purpose announced an international competition for architects, but, however, no final decision could be reached.

In the meantime, various organisations and individuals, especially Father Roth, endeavoured to build a religious monument on the site of so much suffering and such terrible deaths, in order to free it from the deplorable "carnival atmosphere" (*Melbourne Herold*, March 3, 1960) and to substitute a place of silence and recollection, of prayer and atonement for this "rendez-vous for tourists".

This idea was frequently suggested to me also. I gave it my full support and tried to interest others in the project, but I thought that I would have to leave the first step in this matter to others because of my many and varied duties.

Then on the 20th anniversary of the outbreak of World War II on 1st September 1959 something extraordinary happened which forced me to act and to act quickly.

On that very day the world-famous Group-Captain L. Cheshire accompanied by about thirty priests and laymen from England came to the former concentration camp Dachau in order to atone there in nigthly adoration for all the crimes which had been committed there and in many other places against humanity, freedom, rights, health and life.

It was the widely-travelled and active Mrs. Cheshire who said to me during the reception: "*We are very disappointed at the present state of the concentration camp at Dachau.* I have been in all the other concentration camps in Germany and Austria and I have found none in so deplorable a state as that of Dachau. It is so lacking in respect for suffering and death; there is no memorial to remind men of the denial of human rights, the degradation, the deprivation of freedom and the enslavement of hundreds of thousands; no monument of compassionate remembrance for the victims of the godless assaults."

I mentioned various reasons indeed which had hindered the carrying out of the good intentions and attempts of the authorities, but, of course, I could not deny that the criticism was justified.

All the more, therefore, I had to ask myself again and again: "What kind of criticism will there be next year when tens of thousands from all over the world will visit near-by Dachau on the occasion of the International Eucharistic Congress? Before then, something positive and visible must be done, at least a beginning must be made."

And so I began to negotiate with the competent authorities: with the International Dachau Concentration Camp Union, with the Dachau Concentration Camp Priests' Association, with architects and others in order to erect a worthy religious monument, which would be a warning to future generations. Then I looked for co-operators and formed a "Curatorium (Trustees-Committee) for the monument of atonement at the Dachau camp"; opened a special post-office transfer account "Sühnemal KZ Dachau", Postscheckamt München Nr. 20000; looked for a suitable architect and found such a one in Professor Wiedemann from the Technical Academy of Munich. In a very short time he had made the plans for a chapel to be built from stones from the bed of the Isar in the form of a tower at the end of the approximately 330 yards long camp street. This plan won universal approval for its artistic quality and for the idea behind it. His Eminence Cardinal Dr. Joseph Wendel decided that the chapel be dedicated to the Agony of Christ, a reference to the agony which tens of thousands of inmates suffered day and night in this camp. August 5th was the date fixed for the completion of the chapel. It was on the Friday of the Congress Week, the day which was dedicated to the thought of the Cross in a special way, that the dedication was to take place. At the same hour as Our Lord suffered His agony and overcame our death through His death, the sufferings and agony of so many would be remembered in prayer in and in front of the chapel to the Agony.

Although the building of the chapel could be started only at the end of April, it was completed in time, thanks to the energy of the architect Wiedemann and his active partner, Engineer Peither, as well as the building contractors Reischl, the artists, artisans and all the workers.

Soon a great interest had arisen in Germany and abroad. All were interested in the monument and, more especially, in its dedication.

The Catholic youth from Germany and also from abroad made a special "pilgrimage of atonement" to Dachau following a symbolic, expressive programme.

After a Pontifical Mass celebrated by the former prisoner, *Archbishop Adam Kozlowiecki* from Lusaka in Northern Rhodesia, approximately 3000 young men walked from their camps in the tent-city of Munich-Oberwiesenfeld to Dachau, a distance of about ten miles. On the way they sang hymns and psalms, prayed and meditated and carried an old, heavy cross.

The thought of the needs and deaths in the concentration camps of former times as well as those of the Church of Silence in countries of the present day called forth great supplications to our Lord God in song and word:

First, in keeping with the aim and cause of the pilgrimage, the *sad happenings of the twelve years of the Third Reich* were mentioned:

> "Lord Jesus Christ, Thou wast also a prisoner.
> We call unto Thee:
> That Thou wouldst atone for all the malicious deeds of Hitler's Reich by Thy Blood,
> We beseech Thee, hear us.
> That Thou wouldst deign to accept our way as a sign of atonement,
> We beseech Thee, hear us.
> That Thou wouldst deign to unite the sufferings of the tortured and murdered with Thy sufferings and death,
> We beseech Thee, hear us.
> Accept the atonement for the camps in Amersfoort, Auschwitz, Bergen-Belzen, Buchenwald, *Dachau,* Esterwegen, Flossenbürg, Mauthausen, Natzweiler, Ravensbrück, Sachsenhausen, Theresienstadt." A long list of sad names was read, proclaiming great guilt.

The second intention for prayer: *atonement for the especially-bitter persecution of the Jews, for the hatred shown to Jews and other races:*

> "Lord Jesus Christ, offspring of David's house, deliver our people from all enmity against the Jews. Atone for the murder of many millions of the people of Abraham, the destruction of so many synagogues. Put an end to the hatred between the Arabs and the Jews.
> Put an end to the hatred between the Boers and the natives, between the Frenchmen and the Algerians, between the Whites and the Negroes in North America, etc.
> Deliver the White Race from presumption and arrogance Have mercy on the despised peoples . . ."

The third intention of the young pilgrims' prayer was for *those who are persecuted for Christ's sake in our days.*

> "Lord Jesus Christ, since the time of Herod and Nero Thou and Thy mystical body, the Church, are being persecuted in this world. Thy enemies are still vigilant today. They close churches and persecute bishops and priests. They want to turn the hearts of the faithful away from Thee. They want to prevent our youth from learning to know and love Thee. Help our brethren who are persecuted in the whole world, in Russia, Latvia, Lithuania, Hungary, China, North Korea, North Vietnam . . ."

"Peace in the world" is the forth motive of the youth pilgrimage.

"In peace with you, my Lord, my God, let me wend all my ways..."
"Vouchsafe, O Lord, that love and truth, unite us all in Thee..."
sing the youths. Then Psalm 84 takes up this great intention:

"Lord, we call unto Thee: Give peace to the world."

This petition is repeated after each verse, and each continent, yes, each country in which discord and war are or are threatening at the present time are included in this prayer:

"That Thou wouldst grant peace between the East and the West;
That Thou wouldst settle the fighting in Algeria, the Congo, Vietnam, Korea...;
That Thou wouldst preserve our hearts from all enmities;
That Thou wouldst preserve our families, our community, our villages and our cities from all wars."

"Hunger and sickness in the world" is the next need of which the youths think in prayer. First the hymn: "Mary, spread thy mantle out" is sung, then follows Psalm 106 and the following prayer:

"Lord Jesus Christ, Thou hast filled the hungry with bread and healed the sick. We beseech Thee, have mercy on us. Behold the hunger of the nations, give food to those who are hungry. Make us ready to give from our abundance. Call all who are sated to help.
Behold the many who are sick.
Help us to combat leprosy. Help the victims of epidemics, the victims of natural catastrophes, the victims of accidents. Console all who are sick. Let them suffer in imitation of Thee. Heal us from the leprosy of sin. Give us a strong desire for Thy holy Bread."

After this survey of the misery and needs of the whole world, *the youths think of a painful wound of their own people,* the division of their country which is shown even at the International Eucharistic Congress as our brothers and sisters in the East Zone were not permitted to join us in the communal celebration of the Holy Sacrifice.

St. Michael, Patron of the German people for centuries is invoked in the ancient hymn:

"Invincible, strong hero, St. Michael. Come and help us."

After Psalm 32, Mary, the Mother of God, is called upon first and then the saints of heaven who lived and worked on German soil and to whom the German people owe so much: St. Boniface, St. Corbinian, St. Rupert, St. Henry, St. Peter Canisius, Brother Conrad, St. Lioba, St. Mechthild, St. Hildegard, St. Elisabeth and others.

All the needs of their own people are summarized in the petition: "That Thou wouldst grant our people unity and freedom. That Thou wouldst preserve the Faith among our people."

The personal welfare of the youth is the last intention, a petition for their own faithful following of Christ. The hymn:

> "Ye Christians all, O follow Me,
> Speaks Christ our Lord and Hero.
> Take up your cross and miseries,
> Follow My life's example."

gives the lead. Mindful of the powerful propaganda in favour of materialism, the temptation to practical materialism, to avarice and the lust for pleasure, the youths sang Psalm 48, with the following refrain:

> "Do not put your trust in money and in riches, but upon the Lord."

Correspondingly the supplications are then introduced by the thought:

> "Lord Jesus Christ, Thou didst live in poverty. We are in danger of losing ourselves in riches and possessions. We call unto Thee: Be merciful to us. Spare us, O Lord.
> From the danger of riches, from all extravagance, from all desire to possess, from all selfishness, from all discontent . . . Save us, O Lord."

All these seven great intentions were developed in the form of litanies and resounded in silent meditation for a certain time, about four hours.

The thousands who lined the wayside looked on and listened in an attitude of devotion and admiration.

In the camp itself, a crowd of 50,000 awaited the arrival of the young pilgrims. They joined in the hymns of atonement and gazed reverently at the large cross of peace which was carried in front and on the ancient cross from Garmisch which brought up the rear of the procession. After the youths came more than a hundred priests wearing white surplices, priests who had to march on this street in striped uniforms twice a day for years. Then came approximately one hundred bishops and six Cardinals. The solemn chime of bells accompanied this procession, an impressive intimation that the hour of commemoration was to be a religious ceremony.

Canon Reinhold Friedrichs, a former inmate of Dachau, opened the ceremony in the following solemn words:

> "My dear Brothers and Sisters,
> On this ground the Dachau concentration camp was built in the year 1933. Between that time and the end of the war, about 200,000 men, citizens of thirty-seven nations were imprisoned there. It has been estimated that about 30,000 of them died in the camp. They died of contagious diseases, of hunger and exhaustion or they were murdered.
> Over there stood the gibbet on which they were hanged. Some steps farther away the blood of the shot in the neck, ran into the bloodtrench. Behind you lie the

huts in which prisoners were subjected to medicinal experiments which cost many their lives. Yonder were the huts in which the worst punishments were administered.

Fifteen years ago the terror of Dachau came to an end. The disgust, the indignation. the sorrow and shame which it aroused contine. In this hour, there are men assembled here who are unable to forget. There are others, united with them, who dare not forget. There are Belgians, French, Dutch, Israelites, Italians, Poles and citizens of other nations who have suffered in Dachau or whose brethren were tortured and died here. Here present are Germans who once were prisoners in this camp and Germans who lived outside knowing or not knowing what was happening here. What are we going to say and what are we going to do? We are trying to look for an answer to what has happened. We do so as Christians who are mindful of their Lord and Saviour. Christ gave His answer on the first Good Friday in the first hours after noon during which time He underwent the agony on the cross for all the sins of mankind.

We will listen to the witnesses of the concentration camp and the testimony of the agony of our Lord."

Leopold Figl, the former Chancellor of Austria and President of the Austrian National Council reports about his imprisonment and ill-treatment, but also about the consolation and strength which the union with the Passion of Christ and the Eucharist gave to the tortured prisoners.

Then the deacon reads about agony of Our Lord Jesus Christ in the garden of Gethsemane from the history of Christ's Passion according to St. Mark 14, 32 and St. Luke 22, 41 ff.

The bell of atonement sounds, the Bishop prays aloud and tens of thousands join him in the prayers:

"Let us pray for all who have suffered here,
for all who became guilt thereby,
for all who are deprived of freedom and suffer agonies,
for us that we may never become guilty of innocent blood.
Lord, from this place thousands cried to Thee in their distress.
In Thy fatherly love Thou didst not forget them. For the sake of the agony and capture of Thy Son we entreat Thee: forgive us our trespasses, as we forgive those who trespass against us, and lead us not into temptation but deliver us from evil. Amen."

Another former inmate of the Dachau concentration camp, *Archbishop Kozlowiecki*, is given the opportunity to describe the injustices he suffered, his degradation and ill-treatment:

"On November 10, 1939 I was arrested at Krakau and I spent the next five and a half years in prison and in concentration camps: three months in Montelupi prison at Krakau, five months in the concentration camp at Wisnicz, six months in the concentration camp at Auschwitz, four years and four months in the concentration camp at Dachau.

73

I was arrested with my confrère at the Krakau College. Twenty-one of us were subjected to the horror of the concentration camps; thirteen survived, eight were murdered here or in the concentration camp at Auschwitz and their bodies were burned.

Why exactly did they arrest us? This was the first question we asked each other. The Gestapo never gave us a reason for our arrest. No accusation was read to uns during those five and a half years; we were never examined, they did not tell us why we were there.

A watchman gave me a reason once: 'Because you have an ideology which we do not like.' A camp leader said brutally: 'You are dishonourable, defenceless and outlaws.' If at Auschwitz on one day I received only one or two blows, this I counted a lucky day for me. For years, every dark morning we got up with this horrible feeling of agony and absolute help-lessness, it was with a heavy and trembling heart that we went to the morning inspection and to our work.

They tried so kill our souls too. Prayers and religious activity were strictly forbidden. Anyone daring to confess or hear confessions was severly punished."

Again a word from the history of Christ's Passion gave the answer to the question "Why so much suffering?" (Luke 22, 63 ff.; Mark 14, 55 ff.)

The bell of atonement sounds again, the Bishop solemnly invites all to pray:

"Let us pray
for all who were maltreated and tortured here,
for all who are unjustly imprisoned and tortured today,
for all who do injustice rather than suffer it.
Let us pray also that we ourselves are not unjust in our thoughts, words and deeds.
O God, Thy Son once stood guiltless but scourged and crowned with thorns before His enemies. For the sake of His humiliations and sufferings have mercy on all that are deprived of their rights and are maltreated.
Have mercy on us, too, and forgive us our trespasses as we forgive those who trespass against us and lead us not into temptation but deliver us from evil. Amen."

The French Minister of Justice, *Edmond Michelet,* also a former inmate of Dachau, is the third speaker. Speaking ouft of deep experience, he tells how the Eucharist gave power, solace and joy to the prisoners.

"I see the chapel of Block 26; it was closed to laymen of a long period of time. As a Frenchman and consequently 'without any discipline' I went day by day before dawn there. There, we in our hell felt less separated

74

from the external world. In the most real literal sense of the word we were united more intimately with our brethren in the exterior world. Never have I understood so well or with such clarity the deep meaning of the dogma of the Communion of Saints. The poverty of the Polish priests in Block 28 was unbelievable. There was no ornamentation of any sort. The officiating priest celebrated Mass in his prison rags. A thin canister replaced the chalice, a tablet-box the ciborium. But this did not in any way lessen our faith and conviction. We could say with the Psalmist: 'I have loved, O Lord, the beauty of Thy house, and the place where Thy glory dwelleth.' It is indeed fitting that we should have here a chapel dedicated to the agony of Christ and to the Church of Silence. One of our French comrades of Dachau dared to write that those hard years became years of *mercy* to us. How right he was. Is it not an unheard of honour for a layman to be given, all unworthily, the role of a Tarcisius, taking the Holy Viaticum to the patients in the infirmary because the priests had been pitilessly driven away? To my last hour I shall remember the transfigured faces of the dying, their smiles radiant with supernatural joy as I placed on their lips the consecrated Hosts generously entrusted to me by a priest friend . . ." Michelet concluded with Claudel's words: "*O my Master, give me to eat from this Bread. Neither man nor hell, nor God Himself can snatch away Thy Bread which my mouth has received.*"

The deacon now reads from Matthew 27, 39; and 41. 45 ff. and joins this human suffering with the Passion and Death of the Saviour. Another short silence, the bell rings again and the Bishop begins a new prayer:

"Let us pray
for all who were murdered in concentration camps, for their murderers,
for all in this world whose blood cries to heaven.
Let us pray also for ourselves that we never become guilty of the life of another person.
Lord Jesus Christ, grant eternal life to all that were robbed of their life here. For the sake of Thy holy death help us in our dying agony and let us never forget that 'a man cannot hate his brother without being a murderer' (John III, 15). Forgive us our trespasses as we forgive those who trespass against us and lead us not into temptation but deliver us from evil. Amen."

Response:
Cantors: Kyrie eleison, *Scola:* Kyrie eleison.

Ky - ri - e, e - le - i - son.

Now His Lordship, the *Bishop of Essen, Dr. Franz Hengsbach* preached the word of God:

"And being in an agony, he prayed the more earnestly" (St. Luke 22, 43).

"Dear Brothers and Sisters in Christ,

We are gathered here at the hour of the agony of Christ, in the former concentration camp at Dachau, which, only a few years ago, resounded with the cries of agony of several thousand inmates. As Christians we know about the close connection between the agony of God's Son, Jesus Christ, and the various forms of human agony. For this reason our ceremony goes beyond the mere remembrance of what once happened here. It was not for nothing that we were witnesses of how blood innocently shed was revenged by blood senselessly shed during the war, according to the words of the Apocalypse: 'For they have shed the blood of saints and prophets, and Thou hast given them blood to drink, for they are worthy.' (Apocalypse 16, 6).

We have gathered here on the occasion of the International Eucharistic Congress for the dedication of a Eucharistic place of sacrifice, the chapel to the agony of Christ. By completing the consecration that already existed on this site through the blood innocently shed with a consecration based upon the shedding of Christ's Blood, we try, as Christians, to face the horror hovering over this place and over all places for which Dachau – then and now – is a symbol and an example. As Christians we try to find an answer to this horror and to change this place where demons were allowed to rage into a place of blessing, supported by the belief in Him Who broke the power of the demons. The mercy of God is so bountiful that we can even ador Him with our debris and fragments if we only entrust them truthfully to His mercy in order that He may form them into a mosaic.

It is not my intention, dear Brothers and Sisers, to minimize the manifest brutality of this place by investigating the inner circumstances. What happened here was so horrible that it becomes almost understandable that many try not to face the truth, but to forget, to suppress, to conceal and to minimise. Dachau has never exercised grat attraction for us and never will. As we make our way through history, it is more difficult to face up to Dachau than to follow the detours which a bad conscience offers us. Dachau lies before us like an open catalogue of Nihilism. Here the craze for destruction became part of a system of the perfect machinery. Here a collective sadism was let loose and spat into the face of men, beat and kicked them without inhibitions. Here inhumanity became the law of man. It is fatal to fall into the hands of man. We have to consider all this. We have to look at

76

this horror so closely that we no longer can be deceived about the abysses of human fear and misery, brutality and mendacity which still exist in our century of rapid progress of man's knowledge and skill. Otherwise we shall not understand history, shall not understand contemporary man and God's works in the present time.

Which are the inner circumstances? What is there behind all that horror?

It is the defection from God, the prototype of man; the defection from God's Son, Who became incarnate and thus added lustre on mankind; it is the defection from truth, freedom and justice, which are only guaranteed by Him.

This meant that Dachau lost the dimension of reality in which alone man can exist as a human being. Man was nothing more than material, a matter which could be used for the production of soap – this is a diabolic expression of soullessness.

The break with God and Christ was the beginning which led to the perfect and legally sanctioned murder. At the end there was no one to stop the rage of Satan of whom the Bible says: 'The evil one is descended unto you, having great wrath . . .' (Apocalypse 12, 12). In Dachau the devil had erected his throne (see Apocalypse 2, 13).

Dear fellow Christians! We have assembled at the hour of Christ's agony in order to commemorate His agony and the agony of tortured men. The connection between the two is fully explained by the words of the Son of man: 'Amen, I say to you, as long as you did it to one of these my least brethren, you did it to me' (Matthew 25, 40). Interpreting Dachau on this basis we must say: Wherever men go through this agony, the agony of Christ is present. He suffered here. He was hungry, was beaten, hanged, shot, burned. He cried unto His Father: 'My God, why hast Thou forsaken Me?' (Mark 15, 34). He identified Himself with all thoes who fell a victim to inhumanity.

Therefore we cannot commemorate His agony and death without commemorating at the same time the death of His own. Golgotha was present in Dachau just as Dachau was present at Golgotha. Therefore, we cannot celebrate the Eucharist, i. e. spiritually enact the death of our Lord, without remembering the suffering and death of those on whose lives His death conferred a new significance and consecration.

My dear Brethren! What is the concrete meaning of these words? Above all they mean that we have to approach the happenings at Dachau in the same way in which we approach the altar – praying on the altar steps the Confiteor: 'I confess to almighty God . . .' The Gospel reports on the people witnessing the agony of our Lord on the cross: 'And all the multitude of them that were come together to that sight and saw the things that were done returned striking their breasts' (St. Luke 23, 48).

Let us confess as they did: Not only the executioners at Dachau were responsible; not only those who had the power were responsible. In Dachau, as in all other concentration camps, it was clearly shown, as though through a burning lens what exactly man is and of what evil he is capable. We all know more or less clearly that we have our share in sin. This share certainly varies in proportion, be it by commission or omission. We do not want to measure and judge here.

In Dachau our guilt lies open before us. We are well aware of the extreme gravity of guilt we Germans have to acknowledge, since we are responsible for the misery of fellowmen from thirty-seven nations. Just as God knows the guilt of each of us and of those whom we represent at this moment, we confess our guilt to God, to the victims and to each other, our unbounded guilt. Some words from the Gospel on the death of our Lord shall supplement this confession of our guilt. He himself said them on the cross: 'Father, forgive them, for they do not know what they are doing' (St. Luke 23, 34).

We have not only to ask God's pardon, but also that of our fellowmen. Men can only overcome and forgive their mutual guilt by sincere and wholehearted pardon. Therefore the guilty among us ask the victims to forgive us for what was done to them. This applies not only to individuals but to families and peoples in order that through such forgiveness, love may win and triumph over violence. May it be a reconciliation in the spirit of Christ's reconciliatory death at the spiritual enactment of which we pray as He taught us: 'And forgive us our trespasses as we forgive those who trespass against us . . .' (St. Matthew 6, 12).

Still a third word from Holy Scripture must speak for us with regard to what took place at Dachau; they are the words of the Apostle of Nations: 'I rejoice now in the sufferings I bear for your sake; and fill up those things that are wanting of the sufferings of Christ, in my flesh, for His body, which is the Church.' (Col. 1, 24).

Howewer, the admission of our guilt, also the forgiveness we have received or given would be incomplete and imperfect according to Christian principles if they were not followed by our willingness to atone. And atonement embraces here a great deal more than a simple, sincere and generous reparation to the victims and their dependents. Such an atonement is self-evident. It also means more than taking to heart the lessons Dachau has taught us, namely to renounce the spirit of violence, the unbridled use of freedom

78

which alone gives birth to regimes of oppression. Atonement here means sharing the sufferings of the fatally wounded Lord, having the same wounds as He had, atoning together with Him for the wounds of the world. Are there not too many people who not only deny their own wounds but are much less willing to share the wounds of Jesus Christ? They know how to disguise their failures. But as Charles Péguy says: 'God's mercy can never dress the wounds of those who have none.'

The most important point in our willingness to atone is our faith in the power of the grain of corn that falls into the earth, dies and thus bears abundant fruit. For this very reason too, our willingness to atone includes the following: in all our efforts to achieve justice in the world, even – if this must be so – a justice which has to be forced on the lives of peoples and nations; we do not expect salvations to come from force, in the last analysis not even from human justice but from the cross and the mercy of our Lord. This means: We will consider the terrible sufferings which not only as a result of the war but – and this we are inclined to forget too easily when we think of the horrors of war – also as a result of the Nazi injustice were inflicted upon so many of us, on families, groups of people, on nations and on Christian communities as an opportunity sent from God. We will use it as a help in transforming the curse of guilt into the blessing of the cross and to overcome the desire for power by transforming it into the redeeming and delivering desire for imitation of the crucified Jesus.

Dear Brothers and Sisters! Blessed worshippers and great scholars of the Church assure us that in the hour of His agony – during which as we know from Holy Scripture 'He prayed the more earnestly' – our Lord was aware of all the guilt existing in the world. Ever since, Dachau and its agonies are eternally united with the agony of Christ.

One of the thousands of people who suffered here in union with Jesus Christ made the symbol we see before us here: a plain, yet tragically moving monstrance, made from the wood of the misery of these barracks, wood which was worthy to hold in it the Body of our Lord. From this newly blessed site of commemoration may our Lord help us to give the wood out of which our life has been carved such a form that it may be worthy to carry in it His holy Body by the constant spiritual enactment of His agony and the ever present recollection of the agonies of Dachau.

May our Lord give the humble Christian life of each one of us the form of a plain monstrance marked with the agony of the world in which He can appear in this world – He 'the Bread for the life of the world' (John 6, 51). Amen."

Now that the hearts of all are prepared, it is a joy and honour for the auxiliary bishop Neuhaeusler, a former prisoner of Dachau, to dedicate the chapel of atonement which has been built by the sacrifices of so many; to bless the walls and the altar with Holy Water while the choir of young people sings the Psalm 'Miserere'. Touched with emotion the bishop prays:

"Bless, O Lord, this house which has been built to Thy Name. O God, Thou Who dost sanctify the places which are dedicated to Thy Name, pour forth Thy grace upon this place of prayer that all who call upon Thy Name here may experience Thy merciful help, through Christ, our Lord."

To these words is added a silent wish that all who enter this religious monument may call upon the Name of the Lord.

Finally, His Eminence, *Marcello Cardinal Mimmi*, commemorates the 30 000 victims of death in the concentration camp at Dachau:

"Deliver, O Lord, the souls of Thy servants from all burden of sin that they may find rest in the glory of the resurrection among the saints and elect, through Christ, our Lord."

With their gaze directed on the immense crown of thorns above the entrance of the chapel, the tens of thousands, deeply moved, sing:

"O Sacred Head, sore wounded,   What sorrow mars thy grandeur?
Defiled and put to scorn;   Can death thy bloom deflower?
O kingly Head, surrounded   O Countenance whose splendour
With mocking crown of thorns;   The hosts of heaven adore."

Back page: The monument of atonement, a round chapel shaped like a gigantic winepress, built of unhewn rocks and crowned with the crown of thorns. The chapel was designed by Prof. J. Wiedemann, Professor at the Technical Academy in Munich.
Measurements: Height 41 ft. – exterior diameter 45 ft. – interior diameter 35 ft. – Crown of thorns weight 112 cwts – Altar-Block 300 cwts. – Photo: Fruhstorfer